A Field Guide to Visiting a Jewish Cemetery
A Spiritual Journey to the Past, Present and Future

by Joshua L. Segal, Rabbi

Jewish Cemetery Publishing, LLC, Nashua, NH USA

D0905815

A Field Guide to Visiting a Jewish Cemetery
A Spiritual Journey to the Past, Present and Future

by Joshua L. Segal, Rabbi

Cover:
    Upper Left: Gates – Temple Beth Abraham, Nashua, NH
    Upper Right: Shei-mos – Meretz, Woburn, MA
    Lower Left: Monuments – Adath Israel, Massena, NY
    Lower Right: Ne-fesh – North Reading Jewish Cemeteries, North
        Reading, MA

Hebrew Fonts: HebraicaII and NewJerusalem are licensed by Jewish
Cemetery Publishing, LLC from "Linguistic Software."

ISBN(10) 0-9764057-1-7
ISBN(13) 978-0-9764057-1-9

Copyright 2005 by

Jewish Cemetery Publishing, LLC
31 Scott Avenue
Nashua, NH 03062-2443

Second printing 2006
Third Printing 2007

Printed in the United States by Morris Publishing
3212 East Highway 30
Kearney, NE 68847
1-800-650-7888

Dedicated to the Memory of My Parents

Their graves are marked simply as shown in the photograph on the front cover. May they be visited often and be remembered for the many mitsvot of their lives.

פ' ✡ נ'

Here lies	
My beloved husband	בעלי ואבינו היקר
and our beloved father	
Rabbi Solomon Jonathan	הרב ר' שלמה יונתן
Son of Aaron the Levite	בר' אהרן הלוי
Died on 28 Nisan 5725	נפ' כ"ח ניסן תשכ'ה

Rabbi Solomon J. Segal
Died: April 30, 1965
ת' נ צ' ב' ה'

May his soul be bound up
in the bonds of the living.

— — —

Here lies

פ' ✡ נ'

Our beloved mother	אמנו היקרה
Mollie daughter of	מלכה בת
Chayim and Sarah	חיים ושרה
Died on 21 Tevet 5758	נפ' כ"א טבת תשנ"ח

Mollie Segal
Died: January 19, 1998
ת' נ צ' ב' ה'

May her soul be bound up
in the bonds of the living.

A Field Guide to Visiting a Jewish Cemetery

Other publications from

"Jewish Cemetery Publications, LLC"

<u>Available titles include:</u>
A Self-Guided Tour of the Temple Beth Abraham Cemetery, Nashua, NH,
Copyright 2001.

A Self-Guided Tour of the Adath Israel Cemetery, Massena, New York,
Copyright 2002.

*The Old Jewish Cemetery of Newport, A Visitor's Guide to Viewing the
Cemetery,* ISBN 0-9764057-0-9, Copyright 2004

*The Old Jewish Cemetery of Newport, A History of North America's Oldest
Extant Jewish Cemetery,* planned publication 2007

*A Self-Guided Tour of Monuments of Jews Buried in the Mount Auburn
Cemetery Cambridge, Massachusetts* planned publication 2007

<u>Cemeteries as Museums</u>

Jewish Cemetery Publications, LLC will create booklets (such
as some of the self-guided tours listed above) which will turn
your local Jewish cemetery into a museum of local Jewish
history.

**To place an order or for more information or pricing,
contact:**

<u>Jewish Cemetery Publishing, LLC</u>
31 Scott Avenue
Nashua, NH 03062-2443
or
Email: <SegalJL@aol.com>
Web: <CemeteryJewish.com>
Also available from <Amazon.com>

Preface

I have found cemeteries to be interesting places ever since I was a child. The synagogue that I attended while growing up was originally built as a church and right behind the building was the church's cemetery. During the longer synagogue services, children would take breaks by going out to the cemetery. It was exciting to find someone who was born in the 1700s, before there was a United States. It put history into perspective to find the monument of a Civil War veteran. A grouping of children's monuments corresponding to a period of a few weeks, gave a glimpse into the horror of epidemics that ravaged families. Occasionally, a gem of an epitaph would give a fleeting insight into a life well lived.

As I grew older, I would still occasionally visit cemeteries. However, after my mother died, I made a few trips to Jewish cemeteries for pragmatic reasons: I needed to have a monument made for her. What I found was not morbid or spooky. I found mini-museums documenting family histories, Jewish history, and American history.

As my interest in cemeteries grew, I looked around for books on cemeteries. However, the purpose of most available books is to show the artistry of the monuments as opposed to the content of the inscriptions. And due to the limitations of photographic resolution, most of the inscriptions in those books are unreadable.

It is my hope that this book will help unlock the secrets of the inscriptions in Jewish cemeteries. Whether in cemeteries in North America, Europe, or Israel, the Hebrew inscriptions are similar.

Beyond the particulars about the deceased, monument inscriptions include references to the Jewish holidays, the Jewish calendar, the Bible, and more. Since discovering this, I find myself seeking out Jewish cemeteries, for the art, the history, and the culture. This book is designed to help you, the reader, understand and interpret all of these elements. Using this book, you should be able to decode most of the dates and many of the more common inscriptions. For those who would like to dive in without going into the details, Chapter 3, "Monuments 101" is a particularly good place to start, especially for those with minimal Hebrew skills.

The material presented in this book represents the author's observations culled from about 50,000 monuments at about one hundred Jewish cemeteries, mostly in New England.

Acknowledgements

I am grateful to my wife Karen Satz, who helped with the editing and organization of this book. Even more, I appreciate her willingness to wander through cemeteries all over the country, looking for interesting tombstones with me.

Notes on Second Printing:
A number of format corrections and typo corrections were made from the first printing. A few additions were made to the text, index and the list of abbreviations. In addition, an appendix was added that cross-references cemeteries mentioned in the body of the book. Lastly, I acknowledge comments and suggestions made by Judy Fox following the publication of the first printing.

Notes on Third Printing:
An additional topic was added on page 25 titled, Alignment of Graves. Transliterations were changed to the transliteration format of the CCAR "Gates of ..." series. The rational is explained in Appendix F. Appendix G adds an article on pebble usage. Also, many non-Jewish secular decorations find their way into Jewish cemeteries. Appendix H explains many of these. More abbreviations were added to Appendix I and more entries were added to the Index.

1.The Jewish Cemetery

The cemetery as a resource for Jewish culture has been over-looked. Even remote areas, far from the mainstream of Jewish life, have Jewish cemeteries. There was no choice. The first Jew who dies in a region generates a need that demands an immediate response. The following inscription emphasizes the need as it existed in the Netherlands in 1614. Note that it is written in the first person:

In this place	ב"ה [במקום הזה]
I have been turned	קבר העפר התפלשתי
over under the dust.	
In youth, I departed the world.	בצעיר ימים עולם נתשתי
The dedication of *Bet*	חנוכת בית החיים עשיתי
Cha-yim [i.e. this cemetery] I did.	
In the year 5374 by the Jewish	
calendar I departed paradise.	שעד לפק עדן הלכתי
Joseph was the name	
I left behind.	יוסף שמי אשר עזבתי
I was the son to David Senior,	
his name was my pride.	בן לדוד שניאור כשת"י
	[כבוד שמו תפארתי]
In this grave, they buried me[1]	בזאת קבר קברו אתי
in the month of Iyar,	
day two [April 11, 1614].	חדש אייר יומי שני

Over and above the physical need for a cemetery, there is a responsibility to visit cemeteries. Some is motivated purely by the needs of the friends and family to have a place to go to visit a site associated with a person who was important to their lives. Some is associated with the concept of "*ke-vod ha-meit*," the honor of the dead, who deserve to have their remains in a well cared for place.

---

[1] This line is weathered/damaged and is hard to read. If guessed correctly as shown, the Hebrew is questionable.

1

However, in a world where Jewish cultural places are in short supply, visiting a cemetery can be a place to go just to experience Jewish culture, the way we might periodically choose to visit a museum. In a Jewish cemetery, you will see art. Some of it is Jewish, some of it is secular, but it is all clearly in a Jewish setting. In addition, you will see Hebrew. Most of the Hebrew inscriptions repeat often enough to make them reachable by a novice, but some of the more complicated inscriptions can be challenging even for an expert.

Some of the epitaphs give an insight into the life of the deceased. Perhaps, they will motivate some to think, "how do I want to be remembered by a passing visitor in another hundred years?"

Ownership of Cemeteries

From the time that Abraham negotiated for the Cave of *Machpei-lah* with E-phron son of Tso-har (Genesis 23), clear title to burial sites has been important to Jews. Cemeteries are owned in some cases by synagogues, separate corporations, or a *Chevrah Ka-di-sha*. (The Jewish Burial Society, *Chev-rah Ka-di-sha*, literally "holy society" is a group of Jewish volunteers who prepare a body for burial.)

Older Jewish cemeteries often have very small plots for each burial site. This allowed for the obvious economies of selling more plots per acre and lowering the cost per plot to maintain the property. Newer Jewish cemeteries, especially in the suburbs, allow more space per plot. However, as cemetery space becomes more expensive and less available, the number of plots per acre may increase again.

In outlying communities, the cemeteries are often small and isolated. However, in large cities, there is often little space for cemeteries, so extended tracts of land where available are designated to be used as cemeteries. In these cases, many synagogues and Jewish institutions operate and administer sections

2

of these large cemeteries. For example, the Baker Street Cemeteries in West Roxbury, Massachusetts comprises over forty smaller cemeteries.

New cemeteries sometimes form because of local feuds. In a draft document, one synagogue of the late eighteenth century stated:

> If there are people in the community who do not want to make any contribution, and separate themselves from the group, and do not want to support the community, when they die they (sic - their heirs) have to pay for their cemetery lot, as much as the ... Board ... think that the lot is worth. They can demand much or little[2].

When someone dies who is perceived to have owed the synagogue money, the board is in a position to assess a potentially exorbitant price. There are numerous examples of new cemeteries and private cemeteries that have arisen out of this kind of dispute.

In any case, the actual ownership of the plot has always been important as illustrated by the unusual epitaph on the grave of Leon of Modena, a famous Jew of Italy who lived from 1571 to 1648[3].

Four cubits of ground in this graveyard,	ארבע אמות קרקע בחצר הזה
by purchase by kerchief, were from eternity	אגב קנין סודר מימות עולם
transferred from above	הקנו ממעל
to Judah Aryeh of Modena.	ליהודה אריה ממודינה
Here, he hid himself and disappeared.	בזה נסתר ונעלם

---

[2] Marcus, J.R., *American Jewry - Documents - Eighteenth Century*, (Hebrew Union College, Cincinnati, OH, 1959) 96

[3] The Jewish Encyclopedia, Volume 12: Entry titled: "Tombstones", (Funk and Wagnalls – 1906) 192

Cemetery Names and Styles

In Hebrew, the basic term for cemetery is *beit ke-va-rot*, בית קברות, "House of Graves" (Nehemiah. 2:3). However, "house of graves" has a harsh sound to it. As a result, a number of euphemisms have arisen, which include the following:

House of the fathers (ancestors)	*beit a-vot*	בית אבות
House of the living	*beit cha-yim*	בית חיים
House of meeting for all the living (Job 30:23)	*beit mo-eid le-chol chai*	בית מועד לכל חי
House of eternity (Eccles. 12:5)	*beit o-lam*	בית עולם
House of eternity (Aramaic)	*beit ol-min*	בית עלמין

Most Jewish cemeteries are in one of two styles: the classical cemetery or the memorial park. The classical cemetery takes many forms, but the common feature is that monuments are visible and above the ground. The memorial park features ground level monuments. To a passerby, the memorial park looks like an open field. Most classical cemeteries have vertically erected monuments with vertical inscriptions. However, in some cases, a large slab of stone is placed horizontally over the burial site with the inscription on top of the slab.

Where the water table is especially high, as in the Netherlands, or the land is particularly rocky and difficult to dig, like many areas of Israel and North Africa, the terrain prevents bodies from being buried as deeply as they should be. The horizontal slab of stone over the burial site has the added benefit of protecting the burial site from the elements as well as from the

4

local animal population. As people from these areas moved to other countries, they continued using horizontal slabs over burial sites. While the original reason for the custom may no longer apply, this tradition took on a life of its own.

There are cemeteries that are specifically called Sephardic cemeteries[4]. While many Sephardic cemeteries look exactly like Ashkenazic cemeteries, when people refer to Sephardic Cemeteries, they are usually mean cemeteries where the majority of burial sites have horizontal slabs for inscriptions on top of the burial site.

Jews often adapt local customs. Ashkenazic Jews may have been influenced by the majority Christian populations, who use predominantly vertical monuments. The usage of horizontal slabs for inscriptions by Sephardic Jews may have been due to the influence of neighboring the majority Moslem populations especially in North Africa and the Middle East. (These are places where the ground is rocky and difficult to dig, which accounts for why the local populations chose this method and Jewish burial customs copied it.)

Monuments in a particular cemetery may have a characteristic style. This is often driven by local folk art. As you visit more cemeteries, you will pick up on these style variations. In some cemeteries, close to half of the monuments have a cameo photo of the deceased. In others, none do. In some cemeteries a high percentage of the monuments include a ball, an acorn, or an urn at the top (see chapter 4). In others, there are none.

In most cases, there is someone, often the rabbi, who suggests the phrasing or format of the Hebrew for a monument. This results in a common Hebrew idiom from a particular era. Also, the monument manufacturers deal with a particular set of

---

[4] Sephardic Jews are Jews of Spanish and North African origin, as opposed to Ashkenazic Jews who are of German and North European origin. Most American Jews are of Ashkenazi descent.

cemeteries. Each has a set of artwork that they use repeatedly on the monuments they supply. In matching monuments, where one spouse predeceased the other by a number of years, the manufacturer may have changed resulting in lettering in slightly different fonts.

When you visit a cemetery, be sure to pay attention to these elements. Even before exploring the individual monuments, the cemetery's name, the style of the headstones, artwork and lettering will already give you an introduction to the ethos of a community. Not everything described will be in every cemetery[5].

Gates

Cemetery gates may be simple or ornate. Often, their decorations reflect one or more major themes of Judaism, the most popular being the Magen David and the menorah. The Gates of Adath Israel Cemetery, Massena, New York, shown below, include the name of the cemetery and a Magen David.

---

[5] Note that this book is not about visiting a cemetery as a mourner or as part of a funeral. For more on these customs, see Kolatch, A. J., *The Jewish Mourner's Book of Why* (Jonathan David Publishers, Middle Village, NY, 1993).

Sometimes there are one or more biblical quotations on the cemetery gates or even a prayer such as the one that follows (Ouderkerk, Netherlands; Sanhedria, Jerusalem):

Praised be our Eternal God,	ברוך אתה יי אלהינו
Ruler of the world	מלך העולם
who created you in justice,	אשר יצר אתכם בדין
and caused you to live in justice,	והחיה אתכם בדין
and sustained you in justice,	וזן אתכם בדין
and knows the length	ויודע מספר כלכם בדין
of your days in justice,	
and in the future God	והוא עתיד להחיותכם
will resurrect you,	
and raise you up in justice.	ולהקימכם בדין
Praised be the Eternal,	ברוך אתה יי מחיה המתים.
who resurrects the dead.	

Monuments or Tombstones

Cemeteries are mini-museums. While their main purpose is to memorialize those buried in them, they have also become a repository of a very special form of art in the form of cemetery monuments.

These monuments (also referred to as tombstones, headstones, or memorials) offer repetitive themes and artistry. It is important to remember the following:

1. Monuments are not only memorials, they are often objets d'art. A lot of money is spent on monuments. Cost doesn't make art, but in many cases, the extra cost yields extra effort that in turn can translate to a more artistic expression.
2. The more expensive monuments come in very interesting shapes and sizes, which provide variety and contrast to the more simple monuments.

3. Many monuments contain inscriptions that make for interesting reading.

Monuments are a custom, not a requirement of Jewish law. Some suggest that the practice was begun by Jacob, when he set up a pillar on Rachel's grave (Genesis 35:20). Many reasons are offered for the placing of a monument, but the most common is to mark the spot for future visits by friends and relatives of the deceased.

New burial sites may have a monument erected at any time. However, in most cases, people wait about one year before erecting the monument. There are two major reasons offered for this. First, monuments are erected to remember the lives of the deceased. If a monument were erected too soon, it might be considered disrespectful. Jewish folklore suggests that a quickly erected monument implies that the deceased was so insignificant that the survivors were afraid that he or she would be forgotten immediately (Babylonian Talmud, Berachot 58b). The second reason is practical. Monuments tend to be quite heavy. Digging up the ground for the burial disturbs the area around the grave and waiting a period of time allows the ground to settle so that the monument does not have to be reset.

In America today, new monuments are often formally dedicated at a ceremony called an unveiling. A piece of cloth is draped over the monument when the monument is placed in the cemetery. At the unveiling, a member of the family formally removes the cloth. Rabbis are not required but are often present at unveilings.

While there are many rules associated with Jewish cemeteries, there is one overriding truth: there are many exceptions to the rules. Excessive decoration of gravesites with expensive monuments, fences, or special railings is discouraged. Jewish tradition teaches that are all equal in death (based on Psalm 49 and other sources). Therefore, excesses in decoration become demeaning to the poor who cannot afford such luxuries.

Further, if any excesses were permitted, the poor might be tempted to go into debt to provide a "proper remembrance" for their loved ones. Despite this tradition, you will find all of these excesses in some cemeteries. Superlative epitaphs are not supposed to be used in inscriptions. As before, this is also because all are considered equal in death. However, you will find superlatives in some Jewish monuments. (See chapters on epitaphs for examples.)

There are logical reasons for the many exceptions to traditional rules. First, in times of grief, if something provides comfort to a family, sometimes the community will look the other way. For example, this tolerance is one possible explanation for a child's monument in a Jewish cemetery that had a very Christian-looking "guardian angel" engraved on it. Also, sometimes a person who is very wealthy or who has wealthy survivors will ask for something that is Jewishly inappropriate in exchange for a large donation or in consideration for previous donations. Communities sometimes cave in to that kind of financial pressure. Exceptions also occur because in some cemeteries no one reviews or censors the contents of monuments. This may explain why so many monuments have mistakes both in grammar and in content. However, a major purpose of cemeteries and monuments is to provide comfort to the family and friends of the deceased. With that in mind, visitors should be tolerant and nonjudgmental of the things encountered.

Most monuments in Jewish cemeteries are headstones. Footstones were frowned on well into the twentieth century. Arguments against footstones included that they violated the rule that one should not change the customs of our ancestors and that because the head is the most important part of the anatomy, the monument should be closest to the head of the deceased. However, despite these objections, there are footstones in some cemeteries. In some cases, cemetery rules dictate that the headstone has only the decoration and the family name, and that the major inscription be on the footstone.

9

Cenotaphs: Monuments Not to Individuals

A number of cemetery monuments are erected as sculpture for things or people not actually buried there. These monuments are called cenotaphs. Many cemeteries contain patriotic monuments dedicated to those who gave their lives in military service for their country, but the actual remains of the deceased are buried elsewhere.

A number of cemeteries now include monuments to the Holocaust (Shoah). These vary in size, complexity, and themes, but the major themes include the concept of "six," for the six million murdered Jews and the reminder that one and a half million of the Holocaust victims were children.

In North America, these monuments memorialize fellow Jews murdered in foreign lands. In Europe, people remember neighbors, friends, family, and members of their own community. In the cemetery in Ouderkerk, Holland, the inscription reads as follows:

שמן זית זך כתית למאור להעלות נר תמיד

מצבת אבן לזכרון בני קהלתנו אשר הומתו על ידי הצרים

ה תשא - ה תשה

Clear oil of beaten olives for lighting, for kindling an eternal light (Exodus 27:20)
A monument of stone to remember the members of our congregation who were killed by the oppressors
5701 - 5705

Chapels and Other Structures

Beyond monuments, there are many other buildings and structures at cemeteries. Some have tool/maintenance sheds. The larger ones have office buildings. Many cemeteries have chapels for memorial services. These often double as storage facilities when not in use for their primary purpose.

Sometimes, the grave and monument of a noted scholar or leader is covered with a tent-like structure because the monument becomes a site for pilgrimages. Such a shrine is called an *o-hel* (אהל), literally "tent" in Hebrew. In Yiddish, it is called *hoi-sel* (הויזל), literally, "little house."

The "*O-hel*" of Rabbi Jacob Korff, Everett, MA is shown below. The English inscription, shown to the right, is directly behind the menorah.

A fancier stone structure is sometimes referred to as a *ne-fesh* (נפש – soul). The term derives from the kabbalists who believed that the soul continually floats over the grave. The monument provides an area within which the soul has a "physical home." The *ne-fesh* of Rabbi Baruchoff and his wife from the North Reading Jewish Cemeteries, North Reading, MA, is shown below.

Another type of monument that can look like a building is a *tsi-yun* (ציון). While a *tsi-yun* can look like a standard monument, it can also be as large as or larger than a *ne-fesh*. The key difference is that a *ne-fesh* has a door through which one can go inside the monument structure and a *tsi-yun* has no door.

Mausoleums are theoretically against *halachah* (traditional Jewish law). This is because the body is supposed to "return to the earth" (Genesis 3:19). Despite this, you will find mausoleums in some Jewish cemeteries. Keep in mind that some of the structures that appear to be mausoleums are erected after the coffin is already covered by earth and are not really mausoleums.

While not common, there are Jewish burial sites that include both individual family mausoleums as well as community mausoleums. One example of a family mausoleum from the Wakefield, MA Jewish Cemeteries is shown below. The stained glass window on the backside of the mausoleum is shown below on the right.

Burial of Torah Scrolls and other Holy Objects

When a Torah scroll is worn or damaged beyond repair, it is traditional to bury it. Similarly, books and papers with God's name on them and retired pulpit decorations are all considered to have a measure of *ke-du-shah* (holiness) associated with them and it is considered improper to discard these items in a way that does not acknowledge their special status. These items are stored in a *sha-mos* or a *ge-ni-zah* until they can be disposed of in a respectful way, such as burial. A *ge-ni-zah* building in a cemetery in Everett, MA that serves as a storage place until the contents are buried is shown below.

If a synagogue has an upcoming building project that will require digging a foundation, the irreparable Torah scrolls and/or the contents of a *sha-mos* or *ge-ni-zah* are sometimes buried below the foundation. Alternatively, these items are buried at a cemetery in a grave with a noted scholar or occasionally, in their own plot.

What follows is an example of a special plot with its own monument from Meretz, Woburn, MA. The monument is shaped like a book. The left leaf is in English, and the right leaf is in Hebrew. A more literal translation of the Hebrew has been added below and is shown in the right column. The literal translation is reasonably close to the translation presented on the monument.

TRANSCRIPTION		TRANSLATION
REPOSITORY	פ'נ	Here is buried
OF	בלויי ספרים גנוזים	the worn out books hidden away in
SHAYMOTH	שמות	the *sha-mos*
OLD RELIGIOUS OBJECTS	ותשמישי קדושה	along with religious objects
✡	✡	
THE FIRST INTERMENT	זה הקבר הראשון	This is the first interment
ON THE	בבית עולם	in the cemetery
MERETZ RELIEF ASS'N	של	of
CEMETERY	אגודת יוצאי מערעטש	the congregation that emigrated from Meretz
1914	התּרֹעֹד	5674

15

Flowers, Trees and Shrubs

Historically, Jewish graves are not decorated with flowers. Diaspora Orthodox and traditional Jewish cemeteries discourage or do not permit the use of flowers. Liberal Jews generally permit it. Sephardic practices vary from community to community. However, since World War II, individual communities and cemeteries have had varied policies. For example, the Jewish Welfare Board, which approves Jewish chaplains for the military and represents Orthodox, Conservative and Reform rabbis, has ruled that it is permissible to decorate military graves with flowers. In Israel, placing flowers on graves is acceptable.

Most cemeteries allow trees and shrubs in limited quantity, and while they may look nice for a period of time, older cemeteries have many displaced and broken monuments attributable to tree roots and shrub growth. If a newer cemetery has stringent rules against planting trees and shrubs, it is often due to consideration of the potential future problems.

Burial of Jews in Non-Jewish Cemeteries

Jews are sometimes buried in non-Jewish cemeteries. One example is Arlington National Cemetery, where in excess of thirty different religious symbols grace the tops of monuments, including the Magen David. Military cemeteries are often shown with the simple crosses interspersed with an occasional Jewish star. There are simple methods by which the ground for a particular burial site is consecrated as a special Jewish holy spot unto itself. However, the vast majority of Jews prefer to be buried in an exclusively Jewish cemetery.

Burial of Non-Jews in Jewish Cemeteries

The burial of non-Jews in Jewish cemeteries is at the discretion of the rules of the cemetery. Most cemeteries operated under Reform auspices allow non-Jewish spouses to be buried in them, providing there is no non-Jewish service and nothing on the monument or gravesite to indicate that the person buried there was not Jewish. More traditional cemeteries either do not allow non-Jews to be buried in their cemeteries or have a separate section of the cemetery isolated by a fence, wall, or barrier.

Cremation Urns

Jewish tradition does not approve of cremation. At least one reason is that traditional Jewish texts look at the Ezekiel story of the "dry bones" (Ezekiel 37:1-14) as the paradigm for the resurrection of the dead. With cremation, there are no remaining bones that could be resurrected.

Despite this, many Reform cemeteries or sections of non-denominational Jewish cemeteries allow cremation remains to be buried in the same manner as a conventional burial. Some even sell half-plots for urns. Some actually have columbariums with niches for urns. However some have restrictive rules such as burial in a separate section.

Sometimes policy is dictated by circumstances. A small cemetery run by a Conservative synagogue had a "no-cremation" burial policy. A man who owned a plot in the cemetery had relocated out of the area. When he passed away, the survivors of the deceased had the man's remains cremated and returned the urn for burial. The cemetery board met in emergency session to decide what to do. Certainly, if they had been asked in advance, they would have said, no, but in the presence of a grieving family and after the body was already cremated, what could they do? They decided that given the circumstances, it would be insensitive to refuse the burial. They permitted the urn to be buried, but insisted that it be placed inside a regular coffin.

Other Special Sections in Cemeteries

As already discussed, many cemeteries have special sections for mixed marriage couples and cremation urns. While some of these cemetery sections are obvious, there are many more that would be unnoticed without talking to the caretaker.

For example, any association with Communists since the Bolshevik Revolution has had a negative stigma in the United States. A number of Jews affiliated with the Communists. This was especially problematic in the 1950s, with the McCarthy hearings and the Cold War. As a result, at least one cemetery reports that it has a separate section for Communists, but there is no marker in the cemetery to distinguish this section.

Depending on the cemetery, some or all of the following sections exist. While in theory all Jews are equal in the grave, the following list shows that some are more equal than others.

Apostates
According to Jewish law, once a Jew, always a Jew. Therefore, in death, an apostate, a person who formally rejected Judaism, may be buried in a Jewish cemetery as a Jew. However, since apostasy is repugnant to the vast majority of Jews, some cemeteries have a section reserved for apostates.

Children
Children's graves are often placed along an edge of the cemetery. If there are monuments at all, they tend to be small.

Criminals

Based on the Talmudic statement, "the wicked should not be buried with the righteous (Babylonian Talmud, Sanhedrin 47a)," some cemeteries have special sections for criminals.

Leaders and Rabbis

Some cemeteries have a "row of honor" for rabbis, prominent teachers, and community leaders of exceptional status.

Men Only/Women Only

While men and women sit together at services in most non-Orthodox synagogues, Orthodox synagogues do not permit mixed seating. In some Orthodox communities, the custom of separation of the sexes carries over into the cemetery.

Newborns and Stillborns

Jewish custom holds that one is not required to mourn a child who survives less than thirty days. Such a child is categorized with an unborn fetus. A cemetery section for newborns and stillborns is sometimes referred to as a "*ne-fi-la*" (נפילא - Aramaic), the meaning "an untimely birth." The specific usage as "a lot to be set aside for untimely births" can be found in the Babylonian Talmud (Baba Batra 101b). Occasionally, there are monuments in the new born/still born section, but usually not.

In today's world, this may seem harsh. But in the ancient world, childbirth and stillbirth were sufficiently common that the Jewish tradition emphasized getting on with life and living. In the late twentieth century, the frequency of pregnancy has decreased and the percentage of pregnancies that do not end in a viable birth has decreased. As a result, each pregnancy has a greater importance in the life of the family. Responding to the needs and sensitivities of this era, the Reform rabbinate has added ceremonies for miscarriages and stillbirths.

Priests, *Ko-ha-nim*

Because priests (*ko-ha-nim*) are prohibited from visiting cemeteries (Leviticus 21:1-4) except for certain special circumstances, those of priestly descent are often buried near main walkways or thoroughfares in the cemetery. Under certain circumstances, this would allow relatives to attend the funeral who might otherwise follow the prohibitions of entering a cemetery.

Sabbath Observers

Some Sabbath observers (*sho-me-rei sha-bat* [שומרי שבת]) want to be buried only with other like-minded people and there are cemetery sections that accommodate this desire.

Suicides

Judaism values life as the greatest gift that God gives. Judaism teaches that suicide is scorning that gift and is therefore a serious offense against God. For that reason, suicide victims are not permitted to be buried in the main section of many Jewish cemeteries. However, many rabbis rule that only those who are insane would take their own lives. Those who are insane are not responsible for what they have done. Therefore, there was no suicide. If there was no suicide, then there is no prohibition against the individual being buried in the regular part of the cemetery.

What follows is an epitaph from the Chevra Kadisha of Chelsea, Woburn, MA that was in the regular part of the cemetery. One might infer from the phrasing that the burial was for a suicide that was ruled not to be a suicide:

A neglected and pitiful woman,	אשה עזובה ועלובה
forlorn and alone,	גלמודה ובודדה
miserable and childless:	אמללה ושכולה
Miss Leah daughter of Mr. Jacob	מ' לאה בּר יעקב
died of a broken heart	נפ' מפצעי לבבה
21 Marcheshvan 5678 [1917]	כֹּא מרחשון תרע"ח

20

Multiple Burials in Single Plots

When cemetery space becomes unavailable, rabbinic rulings allow multiple burials to use a common site as long as there was a physical separation between the coffins. The separation was defined as six handbreadths (nominally, two feet) (Shulchan Aruch: Yoreh Deah 1. c.3). In the ghettos of Nazi Europe, new cemetery space was unavailable and the existent cemeteries were reported to be twelve sets of remains deep.

The following example of multiple burials in a single plot in Framingham-Natick, MA appears to be a case where space wasn't the primary consideration. Mother and son died within days of each other. Notice that the child appears to have been named after his maternal grandfather.

A young and honorable woman[wife]	אשה צעירה וכבודה
Sima Sarah the daughter of Jacob	שימא שרה בת יעקוב
20th of She-vat 5679 [January 21, 1919]	כ" שבט תרע"ט
together with her son, Jacob	יחד עם בנה הילד יעקוב
27th of She-vat 5679 [January 28, 1919]	כ"ז שבט תרע"ט

In the following example from Montifiore, Woburn, Massachusetts, the child was either not born or stillborn, but went to the grave with his mother without a name of his own.

A woman giving birth	אשה היולדת
Tsi-pah with her son	ציפה עם בנה
Daughter of Mr. Ya-a-kov the priest	בר' יעקב הכהן
Died 23 Kislev 5676	נפ' כ"ג כסלו תרע"ו

Celia Shiler
Died Nov. 29, 1915
Age 24

21

Customs for Visiting Cemeteries

There are certain halachic implications associated with visiting cemeteries. For those who are Orthodox and who may be of priestly descent, *ko-ha-nim* (see section on names), should check with a rabbi before visiting a Jewish cemetery of any sort. Priests are prohibited from visiting cemeteries (Leviticus 21:1-4) except for certain explicit circumstances.

Prayer services should not be held in the cemetery, other than offering an appropriate memorial prayer at a specific gravesite. This rule is based on Psalm 115:17, which says, "The dead will not praise God." Jewish folklore suggests that having a prayer service in a cemetery might be interpreted as taunting those buried there.

Historically, if cemeteries were far from places where people lived, food was often served at or just outside cemeteries. Today, distances to cemeteries are no longer a problem and therefore, food should not be consumed in a cemetery. Like praying, it could be interpreted as being disrespectful of the deceased.

While walking around a cemetery, avoid walking on the area above a burial site. For a close look, the monument should be observed from the side. Otherwise, the monument should be viewed from six or so feet in front of it. If there is a footstone, the monument should be viewed from just behind the footstone. When visiting a gravesite, it is traditional to place a pebble on the monument. Judaism teaches that the guarantee of immortality to the deceased is how they are remembered by the living. Pebbles on a monument show other visitors that the individual buried on that site has not been forgotten. Others argue that the custom of putting pebbles on a monument dates back to a time when monuments were little more than cairns, heaps of rocks often used as a landmark. Placing pebbles on the cairns served to renew them as weather and time eroded them. Still others suggest that in ancient times, bodies were buried in relatively shallow graves. Immediately following an interment, animals would dig persistently in the area. Placing stones and pebbles on the site was done to fill in the holes and to discourage digging by the local animal population. For more on pebbles, see Appendix G.

Some will also drop a clod of sod or grass on a gravesite. One suggested origin of this custom is a medieval superstition that grass keeps away evil spirits. Others base the custom on Psalm 72:16, Psalm 103:14, and Job 2:12, which suggest that grass and earth are symbols of sorrow and resurrection.

Other customs associated with cemetery visits include washing hands and taking a circuitous path home from the cemetery. Both of these have to do with superstitions that demons and evil spirits hover around cemeteries and graves. The water is thought to wash away the demons and the circuitous path would make it difficult for the demons and spirits to follow the visitors back to their homes. Many cemeteries have washing stations at the entrance. In some cases, they are quite elaborate and in other cases, the washing station is just a well-placed spigot.

Solicitors of Charity (*Tse-da-kah* - צְדָקָה)

It is a custom to solicit charity, alms or *tse-da-kah* at cemeteries. The custom is post-Talmudic in origin and is based on Proverbs 10:2, "Righteousness [*tse-da-kah*] saves from death," and Proverbs 11:19, "Righteousness [*tse-da-kah*] is a prop of life."

Be careful not to confuse solicitors of charity with solicitors of money for themselves. There are many larger cemeteries where individuals will prey on the ignorance of visitors, offering to say "the right prayer" for the deceased in exchange for a fee.

23

When to Go

Jewish tradition dictates accepted times to visit a specific monument in a cemetery.

The month of Elul begins one new moon before Rosh Ha-shana and is traditionally seen as a time to visit cemeteries. Often, the local rabbi will be in the cemetery for one or more days of Elul to offer graveside prayers with those visiting the cemetery.

Fast days are considered special days on which to visit a cemetery, because of the penitential nature of fasting. A Jewish concept is that we benefit from *ze-chut a-vot*, the merit of our ancestors. Therefore, praying at a cemetery on such a day invokes *ze-chut a-vot*.

Other times traditionally approved for visiting cemeteries include the days between Rosh Hashana and Yom Kippur, known as the "Days of Awe" or "Days of Repentance." Also, the anniversary of the death of a loved one (*yahrzeit*), the conclusion of the seven-day mourning period (*shi-vah*), and the conclusion of the thirty-day mourning period (*she-lo-shim*) are approved times for cemetery visits. Frequent visits to a specific gravesite are discouraged. This is because the living might be tempted to pray to God "through the deceased." This kind of intercession is considered to border on idolatry.

Visits to Jewish cemeteries should not be made on Shabbat, Biblical holidays including the intermediate days of Passover and Sukkot (*Chol Ha-mo-eid*), Chanukah, and New Moon celebrations (*Rosh Cho-desh*). Several reasons are offered for these prohibitions. First, cemeteries tended to be outside the city, which might be too long a distance to walk on these days, according to Jewish law. Second, there was concern that holidays might have their festive nature diminished by such a visit. Lastly, it might be perceived as taunting the dead to go to the cemetery on a festive day, knowing that the deceased cannot participate.

Finally, visits to a specific gravesite during the first year following a death are discouraged to allow time to heal the feelings of loss. Visiting too frequently could prolong the survivor's pain and prevent healing.

Alignment of Graves in Jewish Cemeteries.
It is clear from many sources, (including Baba Batra 101b) that alignment of graves may be in any direction. Still there are a large variety of customs[6]. A few are listed below:

1. Feet closest to Jerusalem: Nominally head West/feet East:
   Rationale: At resurrection day, the dead will arise and start walking toward Jerusalem (eastward). In this alignment, they will rise facing the correct direction.

2. Feet closest to the cemetery gate:
   Rationale: One can't get to Jerusalem without first leaving the cemetery.

3. Feet North/head South:
   Rationale: The Talmudic states: "When the Messiah comes; all our turnings should be to the right (Sotah 15b)." Therefore, upon rising facing north, a right turn would be eastward.

4. Most cemeteries have as a local custom that all grave sites have a common alignment. However, in a specific case a new narrow strip of land was added to an existent cemetery. The strip could only accommodate additional burials if another alignment was permitted. The alignment change was permitted.

---

[6] Culled from "Direction of Graves in the Cemetery," *Year book, CCAR Vol. XXXIII*, (1923), 58 and *Current Reform Responsa* (HUC Press, 1969) 132ff.

Observations made by the author of various cemeteries would generally support the idea that most cemeteries have a common alignment within the cemetery although not all cemeteries are the same alignment. (That is, some are east-west, some are north-south, and some are something else entirely.) However, there are also cemeteries where there is a central family headstone with footstones surrounding the main headstone, thereby having multiple alignments of graves within a single set of plots.

2. Monument Inscriptions

Reading monument inscriptions in Jewish cemeteries offer a special challenge, since many are written totally or partly in Hebrew and sometimes, other languages as well.

Most monuments include some or all of the following six major parts:

1. Carved decorations.
2. An introductory line or two describing the person, which usually includes the relationship to principal survivors and a few descriptive adjectives
3. The person's name both in Hebrew and the local language
4. The person's date of death by both the Hebrew and secular calendars
5. Something to indicate the age of the deceased
6. An epitaph, ranging from a simple abbreviation to an extensive verse or passage from Jewish sources

Any of these elements can appear on multiple lines and there is no guarantee that each new topic begins a new line. If you are using this book as a guide to understanding the Hebrew on the monuments, don't get discouraged. There are many intricacies of Hebrew as well as errors, acronyms, omissions, and erosion that combine to make understanding all of the inscriptions a difficult skill to master.

If you are stumped, rabbis are usually happy to help with the more complicated inscriptions. Some Hebrew words that appear to be very complex are nothing more than transliterations of place names or family names.

Transliterations

Transliterations are a problem because the rules for transliteration vary. Most of us are familiar with the many variations in the transliteration of the word חנכה, which we've seen spelled Chanuka, Hanuka, Chanukkah, and so on. Transliterating from English to Hebrew is equally challenging, as shown on a single monument with two mentions of the city, Boston, spelled בוסתן in one place and באסתאן in the other. In addition, some transliterated names use Yiddish rules for pronouncing vowels rather than Hebrew rules. Here are four examples:

Chernobel (city in Russia)	טשערנאביל
Chelsea (city in Massachusetts)	טשעלסי
Nightingale (family name)	נייטינגייל
Jacobson (family name)	דגייקאבסאן

Taking Rubbings of Monument Inscriptions

The examples given demonstrate that if you are planning to ask for help on a single word, it is best to write down the preceding and following words to help put the word in question into context. The easiest way to copy material is by taking a rubbing of the area of the monument. To take a rubbing, cover the area of the monument with a piece of paper and rub a crayon softly on the paper[7]. The outline of any lettering or shapes on the monument will appear clearly on the paper. Be careful to completely cover the area being rubbed so that the monument is not defaced in any way. Digital cameras also give excellent resolution for documenting inscriptions if the inscription isn't too badly worn.

---

[7] Note that some cemeteries ban the making of rubbings. If the cemetery has an on site office, check first. Otherwise, look for posted signs.

Inscriptions in Languages Other than Hebrew

People often choose to memorialize themselves or their loved ones in their native language. Jewish cemeteries in the United States include inscriptions in Russian, German, and many other languages. While those are beyond the scope of this book, Aramaic, Ladino, and Yiddish are written with Hebrew characters, so they require special mention.

Aramaic
Aramaic was the spoken language of Jews living in the Middle East several thousand years ago. It has survived in Jewish scholarship, prayer, and songs. Parts of the Biblical books of Daniel and Ezra, much of the Talmud and many midrashic works are written in Aramaic. Well-known prayers in Aramaic include *Kad-dish* and *Kol Ni-drei*; songs include "*Yah Ri-bon A-lam*" on Shabbat and "*Chad Gad-ya*" at Passover.

Monuments sometime include quotes from the Talmud that are in Aramaic, and a few of these are addressed in the chapters on epitaphs. The most common Aramaic that occurs routinely on monuments is the prefix letter *da-let* (ד) which means "of the" or "in the", for example: ב' דר׳ח means "second day of the new moon. (The full abbreviation is dealt with in the section titled "dates.")

Ladino
Judeo-Spanish, also known as Ladino or Espanol, was a language used by Jews of Sephardic descent. It can be written in either Roman characters or Hebrew characters. In general, Sephardic cemetery inscriptions are mostly in Hebrew. There are monuments with extensive Ladino epitaphs, but none are included in this book. However, a few of the more common Ladino terms and phrases are included.

<u>Yiddish</u>
Yiddish was the spoken language of much of the Ashkenazic European Jewish community. Most American Jews have their roots in Europe and do not have to go back too many generations before finding a Yiddish speaker in their family.

While some monuments have Yiddish epitaphs, the "name line" is the most common place for Yiddish. At birth or conversion to Judaism, Jews receive a Hebrew name. However, many European immigrants came to America with Yiddish names and not Hebrew names. Often they gave these Yiddish names to their children as well. The following rules will help in deciphering Yiddish on monuments:

Vowel letters:

alef **א**	"a" as in "ah" or "a" as in "j<u>a</u>w" Note: printed material sometimes clarifies the different pronunciation by using vowels, **אַ** as with "a" as in "ah" and **אָ** as with "a" as in "j<u>a</u>w," but monuments usually do not.
vav **ו**	either "o" as in "c<u>o</u>ne" or "u" as in "c<u>u</u>be"
single yod **י**	"i" as in "h<u>i</u>t"
double yod **יי**	"a" as in "r<u>a</u>te" or "i" as in "b<u>i</u>te" Note: Note: printed material sometimes clarifies the different pronunciation by using vowels, as with **יֵ** = "a" as in "r<u>a</u>te" and **יִ** as with "i" as in "b<u>i</u>te" but monuments usually do not..
vav-yud **וי**	"oy" as in "b<u>oy</u>"
ayin **ע**	"e" as in "b<u>e</u>t"

Consonants:

alef א	At the beginning of a word: it is silent. If a vowel follows, pronounce the *alef* as the vowel that follows. Pronounce as "ah" if no vowel follows.
double *vav* וו	"w" as in "<u>w</u>ater" or "v" as in "<u>v</u>ictory".

Other letters not specifically mentioned above are sounded the same as Ashkenazi Hebrew (i.e. ת is pronounce as "s".) Spelling anomalies also occur, because almost any "sound-alike letters" will be used interchangeably with its correct letter choice. These mistakes occur in Hebrew, but they are far more common in Yiddish, especially as correct Yiddish spellings become less well known.

A number of examples of common Yiddish names are presented below that demonstrate the vowel/consonant pronunciations just described:

<u>Men's Names</u>

Yiddish Equivalent	Trans-literation	Hebrew Equivalent	English	Translation
אייזק	I-zic	יצחק	Isaac	Laughter
בער	Ber	דב	Barney or Bernie	Bear
הירש or הערש	Hirsh or Hersch	צבי	Harry	Deer
העשיל	He-shil	יהושע	Joshua	God is my salvation
וועלוועל or וואלף	Vel-vel or Wolf	זאב	William or Bill	Wolf
יאנקל	Yan-kel	יעקב	Jacob	Held by heel
ליב or לייב	Leib	יהודה or אריה	Judah or Aryeh	Lion
פייבש	Fi-vish	שרגא א (Aramaic)	Phillip	Bright one

31

Women's Names

Yiddish Equivalent	Transliteration	Hebrew Equivalent	English	Translation
בריינא	Bri-na No single equiv.		Brina	Brunette
דאברוש	Da-brosh	דבורה	Deborah	Bee
הינדא	Hin-da	אילת	Ann	Deer
ליבא	Li-ba Female of:	יהודה	Judith	Lioness
פייגא	Fei-ga	צפורה	Fannie	Bird
פרומא	Fru-ma No single equiv.		Fannie	Religiously Observant
ריבא	Ri-ba	רבקה	Rebekka	Beautiful
שיינא	Shei-na	נעמי	Jennifer	Beautiful
or שינא				

Yiddish Inscriptions

Two examples of Yiddish inscriptions are presented. One is straightforward. The other demonstrates the complexities of Yiddish that go beyond Hebrew.

Yiddish inscriptions can be simple as in the following example from Anshe Lebovitz, Woburn, MA. The monument has a book on top with English on the left and Yiddish on the right. We added an additional more literal translation of the Yiddish that demonstrates how difficult the art of translation can be.

English on the Monument	Yiddish on the Monument	Literal translation of Yiddish
Justice his	גערעכטיגקייט	Justice
watch word	זיין מאטא	his motto
the book	בילדונג	education
his world	זיין ליבלינג	his love

Hebrew on inscriptions tends to be relatively true to Biblical Hebrew. However, Yiddish does not have that kind of universal paradigm. Hence, spelling can be inconsistent.

The following inscription from Independent Gold Crown Cemetery, Woburn, MA, is a good example of the challenges of Yiddish inscriptions. It is shown as it appears on the monument from the early 1900's and in another dialect of Yiddish which adds another layer of difficulty to understanding Yiddish monuments.

English Translation	Yiddish in another dialect	Yiddish as copied from the monument
Here rests	אהער רעשט	היער רוהט
in peace,	אין פרידן	אין פרידען
this homemaker,	די א באלעבסטע	דיא בעליבטע
beloved wife	באליבט פרוי	בעליבט פרוי
and mother	און מוטער	אונד מוטער
Tsipa Rebekkah	-	ציפה רבקה
daughter of Nathaniel the Levite	-	בת נתנאל הלוי
died	געשטארבן	געשטארבען
20th day of June	20 טאג יוני	20 טאג אין
Sivan 5676 (1916)	-	סיון תרעו

33

3. Monuments 101

For those wanting to decode most monuments with some Hebrew, without a lot of explanation, this chapter is provided as a stand-alone guide. Each of the chapters referenced below provides a more complete explanation of the specific information presented in this chapter. If the monument doesn't follow the pattern of this chapter, you will need to move to another monument or consult one of the following chapters.

1.	Decoration	See also chapter 4
2.	Introductory Line	See also chapter 5
3.	Name Line	See also chapter 6
4.	Date (including Information on the age of the deceased)	See also chapter 7
5.	Epitaphs	See also chapters 8 through 10

The monument of Mollie Segal is used as the paradigm for this chapter.

1. Decorations:

Magen David

Hands

Menorah

Sometimes the letters: פ"נ pronounced: *Po nik-bar (nik-be-ra)* meaning "Here lies," also appears as part of the decoration as shown in the Magen David above.

The six-pointed star known as the Star of David, the Magen David, or the Jewish Star is one of the best known symbols of Judaism. It is the most common decoration on contemporary Jewish monuments.

The menorah or candelabrum appears on some women's monuments. The lighting of candles is a commandment (*mitsvah*) specifically designated for a woman to perform. Older monuments show these candelabras with two, three, five or seven branches. Some newer monuments use a nine-branched Chanukah menorah, which is counter-intuitive because lighting a Chanukah menorah is not specifically a commandment for women.

For those who claim to be direct descendants from the *ko-ha-nim*, כהנים, "the Biblical priests," the hands are shown at the top of the monument in the position in which they are held when the Priestly Benediction (Numbers 6:24-26) is offered.

In the example shown below, the decoration is the Magen David, with the פ"נ separated by the decoration. The use of abbreviation marks varies greatly from monument to monument and it is shown in the example as פ'נ'.

Other decorations include insignias of fraternal organizations. The most common is the Masonic insignia. Insignias associated with a profession, for example, scales for a lawyer or caduceus for a physician also appear from time to time.

2. Introductory Line
The "Introductory Line" in the 101 version is a simple declaration of survivor's relationship to the deceased. This line sometimes may not appear at all. Examples of the "Introductory Line" include:

My beloved father	A-vi ha-ya-kar	אבי היקר
Our beloved father	A-vi-nu ha-ya-kar	אבינו היקר
My beloved mother	I-mi ha-yi-ka-ra	אמי היקרה
Our beloved mother	I-mei-nu ha-yi-ka-ra	אמנו היקרה
My beloved wife	Ish-ti ha-yi-ka-ra	אשתי היקרה
My beloved husband	ba-a-li ha-ya-kar	בעלי היקר

Some very common "introductory lines" just string two nouns together:

| My beloved wife and our beloved mother | Ish-ti ve-i-mei-nu ha-ye-ka-ra | אשתי ואמנו היקרה |
| My beloved husband and our beloved father. | Ba-a-li ve-a-vi-nu ha-ya-kar | בעלי ואבינו היקר |

The following do not follow the above rules but are sufficiently common to be included here. The syntax is presented in greater detail in chapter 5.

For a man:

| A man of integrity and uprightness. | Ish tam ve-ya-shar. | איש תם וישר |

For a woman:

| An important and modest woman | I-sha cha-shu-vah u-tse-nu-ah | אשה חשובה וצנועה |

In the paradigm, shown also below, the first line is "Our beloved mother, *I-mei-nu ha-yi-ka-ra,* אמנו היקרה."

3. Name line simplest syntax:
The common name syntax is shown below:

a.   b.   c.   d.   e.   f.   g.
Here lies <title><name of deceased><son/daughter of> <title> <parent's name> <last name>

Note that the name does not always start at the beginning of a line. If it is not clear where the name starts, look for a, b or d. At least one of them should be present.

a. Here lies. (Masc.)   Po nik-bar   פה נקבר   פ"נ

   Here lies. (Fem.)   Po nik-be-ra פה נקברה   פ"נ

(Often omitted here if included in decoration.)

b. Title [Sometimes omitted]

   Mister   reb   רב   ר"

   Mrs.   ma-rat   מרת   מ" or מר"

c. Name of the deceased:

Note that there are cases where there is no correlation between the Hebrew name and the English name. While there are potentially thousands of names, the 25 men's names and 25 women's names that follow represent over 70% of the Hebrew/Yiddish names on monument inscriptions.

The Most Common Men's Names

English	Transliteration	Hebrew or Yiddish
Abraham	Av-ra-ham	אברהם
Aaron	A-ha-ron	אהרן
Elijah	Ei-li-ya-hu	אליהו
Eliezer	E-li-e-zer	אליעזר
Aryeh (Ari)	Ar-yei (A-ri)	אריה (ארי)
Benjamin	Bin-ya-min	בנימין
Dov	Dov	דוב (דאב)
David	Da-vid	דוד
Hirsch	Hirsch	הירש (הערש)
Wolf (William)	Ze-eiv	זאב
Chaim (Hyman)	Cha-yim	חיים
Judah	Ye-hu-da	יהודה
Joshua	Ye-ho-shu-a	יהושע
Joseph	Yo-seiph	יוסף
Jacob	Ya-a-kov	יעקב
Isaac	Yits-chak	יצחק

English	Transliteration	Hebrew or Yiddish
Israel	Yis-ra-eil	ישראל
Leib	Leib	לייב
Meyer	Mei-ir	מאיר
Michael	Mi-cha-eil (Mi-chel)	מיכאל (מיכל)
Mordecai	Mor-de-chai	מרדכי
Moses	Mo-she	משה
Tsvi	Tse-vi	צבי
Solomon, Zelman	She-lo-mo, Zel-man	שלמה (זלמן)
Samuel	She-mu-eil	שמואל

The Most Common Women's Names

English	Transliteration	Hebrew or Yiddish
Etta	E-ta	אטא, איטא, איטע, עטע...
Esther	Es-ter	אסתר
Belle	Bei-leh	ביילה, ביילע
Brina	Bri-na	ברײנה, ברײנע
Basha	Ba-sha	בתיה, באסיה, באשא
Golda	Gol-da	גאלדא
Gittel	Gi-tel	גיטל, גיטאל, גיטעל
Deborah	De-vo-ra	דבורה
Henna	He-neh	הינה, העננע, הענא, היענע
Chaya	Cha-ya	חיה
Hannah	Cha-na	חנה
Leah	Lei-ah	לאה
Libby	Li-ba	ליבא, ליבע
Minnie	Mi-na	מינא, מינע, מאניע, מיניה
Mollie	Mal-kah	מלכה
Miriam	Mir-yam	מרים
Ethel	E-tel	עטיל, עטל
Fay	Fei-ge	פײגה, פײגע, פיגא...
Pesha	Pe-si	פעסי, פעשה, פעסיע, פסיה...
Freida	Frei-da	פרײדא, פרײדע

Rebecca	Riv-kah	רבקה
Rachel	Ra-cheil	רחל
Rose, Risa, etc.	Rei-zel	ריזל, רייזל, רייזעלע,
		רייצעל, רייזיל, ריסע...
Shana	Shei-na	שיינה
Sarah	Sa-rah	שרה

Notice that the spelling of Yiddish names varies greatly. In some cases, multiple spellings are shown, but a general rule is that the following letters or letter combinations are sometimes used interchangeably. (While grammar experts may argue otherwise, these results are based on empirical observations.) א and ה and ע; ב and וו; ז and צ and ס and ש; ח and כ; ט and ת; י and יי and וי.

A middle name may also be included, but it is not in our paradigm. The name in our paradigm is "Mal-kah, מלכה", which corresponds precisely to the English name, Mollie.

d. Relationship (Son/Daughter of...)

| Son of | Ben | בן | |
| Son of Mister ... | Ben reb (Bar) | בן רב | "בר |

| Daughter of | Bat | בת | |
| Daughter of Mister | Bat reb (Bar) | בת רב | "בר |

In our paradigm above, Mollie, "Daughter of (Bat, בת)".

e. Title of parent:
The titles of the parent are exactly the same as the titles of the deceased and were described in b., above.

In our paradigm, there are no titles.

f. Parent's name:
Traditionally, the only parent mentioned on the monuments was the father. This is still the case in most Orthodox cemeteries. Reform and some Conservative cemeteries now include both the father and mother's name. This is the case in our paradigm, which identifies "Mal-kah as the daughter of Cha-yim and Sa-rah."

g. Last name (surname):
The last name is usually a transliteration. It often does not appear at all or may stand alone on the following line. In our paradigm, it does not appear.

4. Dates

Like the names, dates do not always start on a new line. Also, dates are not limited in length to a single line. The easiest way to find the date line is to look for "נ‎פ, (short for *nif-tar,* נפטר, or *nif-te-ra,* נפטרה, meaning he or she died) and the date will follow. If the "נפ is missing, a way to find the date line is as follows: if the date of death is 1940 or later, look for an abbreviation beginning with תש. If the date of death is between 1840 and 1940, look for an abbreviation beginning תר.

Generic Example:

| a. | b. | c. | d. | | d. | c. | b. | a. |

Died <day><month><year>   <year><month><day> "נפ

Specific paradigm:

| | d. | c. | b. | a. |

נפ' כ"א טבת תשנ"ח

a. b. c. d.
Died 21 Tei-vet 5758   נפ' כ"א טבת תשנ"ח

See Table 1 for days, Table 2 for Months and Table 3 for years.

Table 1: days

Note that below, all numbers are shown with quotes as the abbreviation mark. Sometimes, other marks are used for abbreviations including an apostrophe, a dot, a tilde or even.

1	א"	11	י"א	21	כ"א
2	ב"	12	י"ב	22	כ"ב
3	ג"	13	י"ג	23	כ"ג
4	ד"	14	י"ד	24	כ"ד
5	ה"	15	ט"ו	25	כ"ה
6	ו"	16	ט"ז	26	כ"ו
7	ז"	17	י"ז	27	כ"ז
8	ח"	18	י"ח	28	כ"ח
9	ט"	19	י"ט	29	כ"ט
10	י"	20	כ"	30	ל"

Table 2: months

Tish-ri	תשרי	A-dar Bet or	אדר ב'
Chesh-van	חשון	A-dar Shei-ni or	אדר שני or
or Mar-chesh-van	מרחשון or	or ve-a-dar	ואדר or
Kis-leiv	כסלו	Ni-san	נסן
		or A-viv	אביב or
Tei-veit	טבת	I-yar	אייר
She-vat	שבט	Si-van	סיון
A-dar	אדר	Tam-muz	תמוז
or A-dar A-lef	אדר א' or	Av or Me-na-chem Av	אב
			מנחם אב or
or A-dar Ri-shon	אדר ראשון or	E-lul	אלול

43

Table 3: years

Most monuments have the common calendar year on them. You can compute the Hebrew calendar year (usually given by a string of Hebrew letters) using the following equations:

If the common calendar year ends in an even number and
1. If the Hebrew year ends in טו add 3760.
2. If Hebrew year ends in א, ג, ה, ז(except טו), טז or ט add 3761.
3. In all other cases, add 3760.

If the common calendar year ends in an odd number and
1. If the Hebrew year ends in טו add 3761.
2. If the Hebrew year ends in א, ג, ה, ז(except טו), טז or ט add 3760.
3. In all other cases, add 3761.

Examples of computation of the year:
Example 1 (from paradigm):
נפ' כ"א טבת תשנ"ח January 19, 1998
The common calendar year, 1998 is even. The Hebrew date ends in ה. The letter is not on the list. 1998+3760=5758.

Example 2 (a random date):
נפ' ג' חשון תשל"ה October 19, 1974
The common calendar year, 1974 is even. The date ends in ה. The letter is on the list. 1974+3761=5735.

Note: More than 80% of the time, the age of the deceased can be determined from the monument, but usually, not from the Hebrew or Hebrew dates.

5. Epitaph

Epitaphs can be long and complicated. However, a large majority of monuments have one of the following three choices as their epitaph.

Let his (her) soul	Te-hi naf-sho	תנצב"ה
be bound up	(naf-sha) tsa-ru-ra	
in the bonds of the living.	be-tse-rur ha-cha-yim.	
(Adapted from1 Sam. 25:29)		

May his(her) memory	Zich-ro-no (Zich-ro-na)	ז"ל
be a blessing	Le-ve-ra-cha	
. (Based on Prov. 10:7)		
May the memory	Zei-cher tsa-dik	זצ"ל
of the righteous		
be a blessing (Prov. 10:7)	Le-ve-ra-cha	

Many Jews believe in the concept of "life after death" or a "World to Come". However, from the point of view of Jewish theology, there are no guarantees. The only guarantee is that we will be remembered by the living for those things we did in our lifetimes. This is the message reflected in the acronyms תנצב"ה, ז"ל and זצ"ל.

In the paradigm for this chapter, the first example of the epitaph is shown:

Full Example

Here lies	פ"נ
our beloved mother	אמנו היקרה
Mollie daughter of	מלכה בת
Cha-yim and Sa-rah	חיים ושרה
Died on 21 Tei-vet 5758	נפ' כ"א טבת תשנ"ח
	MOLLIE SEGAL
	DIED: JANUARY 19, 1998
May her soul be bound up	ת נ צ ב ה'
in the bonds of the living.	

A Worksheet for Monuments 101:
Example

פ' ✡ נ'

Line 1:	Here lies
Line 2:	My beloved husband	בעלי ואבינו היקר
	and our beloved father
Line 3:	Yits-chak son	יצחק בר' יעקב
	of Mister Ya-akov
Line 4:	Died 28 Nisan 5734	נפ' כ'ח ניסן תשל'ד
Line 5:	Let his soul be bound	תנצב'ה'
	up in the bonds of the living.

April 20, 1974

1.   נ' <decoration: _____> פ'
      Likely options: Magen David, Menorah, Hands

2. Introductory Line _____

3. Name   _____

4. Date of death   Year   Month   Day

_____|_____|_____ נפ'

5. Epitaph

תנצב'ה' or ז'ל or זצ'ל or

_____

47

4. Tombstone Art

Decoration:	פ ✡ נ
Introductory Line:	אבינו היקר
Name Line:	יצחק בן יוסף
Dateline:	נפ" כ"ח ניסן תשל"ז
	Isaac Stone
	Died April 16, 1977
Epitaph:	תנצב"ה

Occasionally, a monument is just a stone with writing. Yet the choices associated with the lettering have an artistic element. What size are the letters? What font is used? Letters can be either positive (letters raised above the background) or negative (letters cut below the background). But in most cases the monument has decorations that augment the artistic merit. Many of the decorations and motifs found on monuments are described in this chapter.

While this chapter provides a lengthy list, 95% of all Jewish monuments will have either no decorations or one of the following four: Candelabra, Magen David, Hands or Pitcher.

Menorot or Candelabras

Lighting candles is a commandment (mitsvah) specifically designated for women to perform. As a result, a menorah (plural: me-no-rot) or candelabra is often a decoration on a woman's monument, as shown below.

Older monuments show these candelabras as having 2, 3, 5 or 7 branches. Some newer monuments use a nine-branched Chanuka menorah, which is counter-intuitive since lighting a Chanuka menorah is not a commandment specifically for women.

Star of David, Jewish Star or Magen David

The six-pointed star is often thought to be the symbol of Judaism. It is the most common decoration on Jewish monuments.

The Hebrew letters, "*pei*" and "*nun*" are shown inside the star. These letters are an abbreviation for "*po nik-bar*", meaning: "here lies". [This abbreviation is discussed in greater detail in Chapter 6.]

There are many variations of the star above including the following:

1. Instead of פ׳נ, inside the star, the "pei", "nun" will appear on either side of the star.
2. Instead of פ׳נ, *tsi-yun*, meaning "monument" (ציון), will appear inside the star. [It is easy to mistake this word for its homograph, *Tsi-yon* meaning "Zion".]
3. The letters תנצב׳ה meaning "Let his (her) soul be bound up in the bonds of the living" (see chapter 8, "Epitaphs" for more detail) will appear counterclockwise inside the outer points of the star with the bottom point left blank.

Hands

For those descended from priests [*ko-ha-nim*, כהנים], the hands are shown at the top of the monument in the position in which they are held when the priestly blessing (Numbers 6:24-26) is offered. (See Chapter 6:2.c. "Name Descriptors" for more details).

People with last names "Cohen, Kagan, Kahn, Kaplan and Katz" often will have the hands of the priest on their monument. This symbol is usually only on a man's grave, because daughters of priests did not participate in offering the priestly blessing.

Pitcher

Levites were historically the assistants to the priests. On many monuments of descendants of Levites, the Levite is shown holding a pitcher with which he would help the priest wash his hands in preparation to give the priestly blessing. (See Chapter 6, 2.c. "Name Descriptors" for more details).

People with last names "Levine, Levy, and Segal" often will have the pitcher on their monument. This symbol is usually only on a man's grave, because daughters of Levites did not participate in offering the priestly blessing.

Eternal Light or Flame

The eternal light is a more modern decoration. Its message appears to be "eternal memory." This symbolism could be related to the "*Ner Tamid*" or Eternal Light that is used symbolically in most synagogues. However, most examples of this decoration that I found post-date the assassination of President John Kennedy whose monument includes an eternal flame. Therefore, I have reason to believe that the symbolism was drawn from the greater American society as much as from Jewish culture.

Decorations Related to the Name of the Deceased

The following is a partial list of decorations that appear on monuments of people who have specific names.

Bear - The name of the person buried is Dov (דוב) or Yiddish, Baer (בער)

Cockerel (Young rooster) - Hahn (Yiddish: האן)

Deer - The name of the person buried is Tsvi (צבי) or Yiddish, Hirsch (הירש or הערש)

Dove - The name of the person buried is Jonah (יונה)

Fish - Family name Fish, Fischel, Karp or profession of fisherman (Yiddish: קארפ)

Fox - Family name Fuchs or Fox (Yiddish: פוקס)

Goose - Family name Gans (Yiddish: גאנדז)

Lions -

> 1. The name of the person buried is Judah (יהודה) or Yiddish, Leib (לייב)
>
> 2. The name of the person buried is "Aryei"(אריה), meaning lion

Mouse - Family name Meisel (Yiddish: מויזל)

Polecat (skunk) - Family name Iltis (Yiddish: אילטיס)

Scissors - Family name Tailor or Taylor (Yiddish: Schneider: שניידער)

Wolf - The name of the person buried is Wolf (זאב) or Yiddish, וואלף.

Decorations Related to the Profession of the Deceased

The following is a partial list of decorations that appear on monuments of people who have specific professions.

Book - bookbinder or scholar
The example below, with a Torah and books, was on the monument of a rabbi.

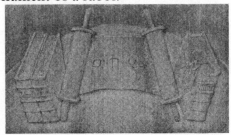

Caduceus - physician
Circumcision instruments - mohel
Lancet - physician
Mortar – chemist, apothecary
Musical notes - musician
Neck chain - jeweler
Palate - artist, painter
Quill - scribe, family name Sofer
Retort - Chemist
Scales (as in scales of justice) - Attorney
Scissors – Tailor or Taylor
Violin – musician

Other Symbolic Images

Grape - Wisdom and/or fertility
Lions -
    1. Common symbol of Judaism
    2. Symbol of tribe of Judah

53

Decorations Related to the Organizations to which the Deceased Belonged

People take pride in the organizations to which they belonged. Some monuments include the name of the synagogue to which the deceased belonged. Beyond that, the following is a partial list of decorations that appear on monuments of people who belonged to specific organizations.

Civic and Fraternal Organizations: e.g. International Order of Odd Fellows (IOOF), Jewish War Veterans (JWV).
Eastern Star - a five-pointed star on the monuments of some spouses of Masons.
Masonic Insignia - mason.

Military Insignias of all sorts
Seals of cities, states, etc.
Shriner's Insignia - subset of the Masons.
Workman's Circle - "AR" surrounded either by a Jewish Star or logo. "AR" stands for "Arbeiter Ring"
(פאלקס ארבעטער)

Decorations Related to Positive Traits of the Deceased

The following is a partial list of decorations that describe what is more often stated in the epitaph.

Crown - crown of a good name
Money box - symbol of charitable person
Ten Commandments - scholar
Torah - scholar or rabbi

54

Biblical Scenes

Biblical scenes of all sorts may appear, often related to the name of the person. Scenes include Garden of Eden imagery (Gen. 2:8ff) and ladders to heaven (Gen. 28:12). Gates at the top of the monument are likely to be the "gates of heaven" (Gen. 28:17 inter alia).

Open Book

An open book, probably symbolic of the "Book of Life," appears on many monuments. Sometimes, there is writing inside the book and sometimes just the shape of the book is used as an indication that the deceased was a scholar. The example below is one way words are arranged on the open book.

Here	is rest	מנוח	פה
for the weary	with the help of God.	ב"ה	ליגיע
Let the dirt	of the grave	קבר	רגבי
be sweet	to the gentleman. (I.e. Rest in Peace.)	לגבר	ימתקו

Other Decorations

Other decorations include floral ornaments, floral vases, flowers, four leaf clovers, fruit, garlands, heart-shapes, stars (other than 6 pointed) and weeping willows. They are thought to be derived from local folk art. See Appendix H for a listing of the interpretation of many of these folk art symbols. Many monuments have an initial of the family name in a circle at the top.

Newer cemeteries include engravings of dogs or cats, in many cases reflective of the deceased's pet(s) or love for a pet. Butterflies and birds are based on a theme of a free spirit.

Small boxes in front of the monument are for *yahrzeit* or memorial candles. Newer cemeteries have containers for flowers as well as containers for pebbles. (See Chapter 2 and Appendix G for more on pebbles.)

A cameo photograph of the deceased became common as photographic technology became available. A disproportionate number of these are faded, stolen or vandalized. Below is a typical photograph of a grouping of monuments with vandallized or missing cameo photos from Everett, MA.

Some of these cameo photographs have hinged covers, which usually preserves the photo in better condition. One monument even advertised:

| This is a picture of | Zot te-mu-nat | זאת תמונת |
| my beloved wife. | i-sha-ti ha-yi-ka-ra | אשתי היקרה |

Some will argue that photos are "engravings of human images" and as such are a violation of the second of the Ten Commandments (Exodus 20:4, Deuteronomy 5:8). While photographic likenesses are common, engraving the photograph on the monument was not easily done. Today, newspapers use "dot density technology" for making images on paper with only black and white. The same method can be used on monuments, and sometimes it is. Many would argue that such images are truly "graven images" and more improper than photographs. Proper or not, both exist.

Sign language hand positions also appear. The one shown above means "I love you," which at first glance looks like the letter, "shin."

Monument Tops

Many of the monument tops shown and described below are more generic cemetery art than specifically Jewish cemetery art. In some cemeteries they are common. In others, there are no monument tops.

A. Acorn
An acorn becomes a great oak only after it is buried. It symbolizes afterlife.

B. Ball
A ball is the perfect shape with no beginning and no end, symbolizing eternity.

C. Jug
The jug is symbolic of the body which is the container for the eternal soul.

Children's Monuments

Children's monuments are often small. The lamb, which has the symbolism of youth and purity, is a common decoration on a child's monument. Other engravings include birds, pets and even toys. The most common symbolism is a tree or broken off tree, indicating the person was cut off before his or her time. Along the same theme is a piece of chain, indicating that the link of family continuity is broken.

There are many sad stories associated with death and especially the death of a child. One of the more powerful stories came from a child's monument. It is a broken off tree as shown below, with a *Chanukiyah* (Chanukah Menorah) at the top. The seven-year-old died on the 5th day of Chanukah, 1928. (North Russell St. Shul, Everett, MA.)

5. Introductory Hebrew Line

Decoration:	פ ☆ נ
Introductory Line:	אבינו היקר
Name Line:	יצחק בן יוסף
Dateline:	נפ" כ"ח ניסן תשל"ז
	Isaac Stone
	Died April 16, 1977
Epitaph:	תנ'צ'ב'ה'

The "Introductory Hebrew line," as I have chosen to title it, is a phrase or two briefly describing the person. Most often it mentions the relationship of the deceased to principal survivors as well as a few descriptive adjectives. It does not appear on all monuments and when it doesn't, it can make the monument more difficult to parse. Complicating this problem is that the epitaph occasionally appears in this position. If the material described in this chapter doesn't match the material on the monument being examined, try to relate this line of the inscription to the chapters on epitaphs.

This chapter is divided into four parts corresponding to four different types of "Introductory Hebrew Lines." They include:
1. The active voice format relative to survivors. Example: Our beloved...
2. The passive voice format relative to survivors. Example: He/She was beloved to his/her ...
3. A format that very briefly describes the deceased just before mentioning his/her name. Example: A compassionate physician, <name of deceased>...[8]

---

[8] The distinction between this format and an epitaph is somewhat arbitrary. The author suggests that if the material leads directly to the name of the deceased, that it is in the category of "Introductory Hebrew Line" and if it does not lead directly to the name of the deceased, it is categorized as an epitaph.

4. An introductory statement about the monument. Example:
For the perpetual memory of <name of deceased> …

Active voice format relative to survivors:

The format that is the most common on monuments is as follows:

1. Our beloved father...   A-vi-nu ha-ya-kar ...   ...אבינו היקר
   Several other examples this form are:

2. My beloved husband   Ba-a-li ve-a-vi-nu   בעלי ואבינו היקר
   and our beloved father.   ha-ya-kar.

3. My beloved and   I-sha-ti ha-yi-ka-ra.   אשתי היקרה
   modest wife.   ve-ha-tse-nu-a   והצנועה

The general syntax of the above "introductory Hebrew line" examples are as follows:

    a. <Descriptive relationship or noun, usually with a pro-
    nominal suffix>
    b. <one or more adjectives describing the individual>
    c. <name line (see chapter 6)>
    (The "Introductory Hebrew Line" flows into the "name
    line", represented above as c.<name line>.)

When more than one relationship or adjective is specified the words may be linked with the letter vav (ו), meaning "and" as shown in examples 2 and 3 above.

a. Vocabulary: <Descriptive relationship or noun, usually with a pronominal suffix>

Nouns
My father   A-vi   אבי
Our father   A-vi-nu   אבינו
My beloved   A-hu-va-ti אהובתי

My sister	A-cho-ti	אחותי
Our sister	A-cho-tei-nu	אחותינו
My brother	A-chi	אחי
Our brother	A-chi-nu	אחינו
My husband	I-shi	אישי
My mother	I-mi	אמי
Our mother	I-mei-nu	אמנו
My wife	I-sha-ti	אשתי
My son	Be-ni	בני
Our son	Be-nei-nu	בננו
My husband	Ba-a-li	בעלי
My daughter	Bi-ti	בתי
Our daughter	Bi-tei-nu	בתנו
My beloved (husband)[9]	Do-di	דודי
My beloved (wife)[10]	Do-da-ti	דודתי
My wife (My mate)	Zu-ga-ti	זוגתי
Our Grandfather	Zik-nei-nu	זקננו
Our Grandmother	Zik-na-tei-nu	זקנתנו
My friend	Cha-vei-ri	חברי
Our friend	Cha-vei-rei-nu	חברנו
My teacher	Mo-ri (Mo-ra-ti)	מורי (מורתי)
Our teacher	Mo-rei-nu (Mo-ra-tei-nu)	מורנו (מורתנו)
My grandchild	Nech-di	נכדי
My wife (My companion)	Ra-ya-ti	רעיתי

---

[9] Could also be translated as "my uncle" but the monument's context won't generally support that translation.

[10] Could also be translated as "my aunt" but the monument's context won't generally support that translation.

b. Vocabulary: <one or more adjectives describing the individual>

Adjectives or Nouns Used as Adjectives

Note: This list of adjectives applies to all of the other formats presented later in the chapter.

The list is organized by the Hebrew alphabet in the right-most column. Masculine adjectives with the direct object include the same word as the right-most column but adds the "ה" of the definite article (i.e. "the"). A similar column for feminine adjectives was omitted for simplicity.

Translation	Feminine Transliteration	Feminine	Masculine with direct object	Masculine Transliterati	Masculine Adj or noun
Loved	a-hu-va	אהובה		a-huv	אהוב
Man (Woman) of valor	ei-shet cha-yil	אשת חיל		ish cha-yil	איש חיל
Truthful or trustworthy				e-mu-na	אמונה
Truthful or trustworthy				e-mu-nim	אמונים
Pure	za-cha	זכה	הזוך	zach	זך
Dear one				chi-ba	חבה
Dear one of				chi-bat	חבת

Translation	Feminine Transliteration	Feminine	Masculine with direct object	Masculine Transliteration	Masculine Adj or noun
Dear one	cha-vi-va	חביבה	החביב	cha-viv	חביב
Valor				cha-yil	חיל
Pleasant	cha-mu-da	חמודה	החמוד	cha-mud	חמוד
Righteous	cha-si-da	חסידה	החסיד	cha-sid	חסיד
Important	cha-shu-va	חשובה	החשוב	cha-shuv	חשוב
Wise				cha-cham	חכם
Good	to-va	טובה	הטוב	tov	טוב
Good hearted				tov leiv	טוב לב
Beloved	ye-di-da	ידידה	הידיד	ye-did	ידיד
Beloved	ye-ka-ra	יקרה	היקר	ya-kar	יקר
Beloved				ye-kar ru-ach	יקר רוח
Beloved	ya-ki-ra	יקירה	היקיר	ya-kir	יקיר

Translation	Feminine Transliteration	Feminine	Masculine with direct object	Masculine Transliteration	Masculine Adj or noun
Honest	ye-sha-ra	יְשָׁרָה	הַיָּשָׁר	ya-shar	יָשָׁר
Honor or honorable	ki-vo-da	כְּבוּדָה	הַכָּבֵד	ki-vod or ki-bud	כָּבוֹד
Mighty	ka-bi-ra	כַּבִּירָה	הַכַּבִּיר	ka-bir	כַּבִּיר
Priest	co-he-net כֹּהֶנֶת or כֹּהֶנֶת		הַכֹּהֵן	co-hein	כֹּהֵן
Daughter of a priest					
Proper	ke-sha-ra	כְּשֵׁרָה	הַכָּשֵׁר	ka-sher	כָּשֵׁר
Levite			הַלֵּוִי or הַלֵּוִי	lei-vi	לֵוִי or לֵוִי
Prominent	muf-la-ga	מֻפְלָגָה	הַמֻּפְלָג	muf-lag	מֻפְלָג
Delight	mach-me-da	מַחְמְדָה	הַמַּחְמָד	mach-mad	מַחְמָד
Prominent or famous	me-fur-se-met	מְפֻרְסֶמֶת	הַמְפֻרְסָם	me-fur-sem	מְפֻרְסָם
Faithful	ne-e-ma-na	נֶאֱמָנָה	הַנֶּאֱמָן	ne-e-man	נֶאֱמָן
Benefactor, philanthropist				nad-van	נַדְבָן
Generous	ne-di-va	נְדִיבָה	הַנָּדִיב	na-div	נָדִיב
Generous				ne-div leiv	נְדִיב לֵב

Translation	Feminine Transliteration	Feminine	Masculine with direct object	Masculine Transliteration	Masculine Adj or noun
Lovely	nech-me-da	חמדה	הנחמד	nech-mad	נחמד
Honored	nech-be-da	נכבדה	הנכבד	nech-bad	נכבד
Pleasant	ni-i-ma	נעימה	הנעים	na-im	נעים
Superior, exalted	na-a-la	נעלה	הנעלה	na-a-leh	נעלה
Noble	a-di-na	עדינה	העדין	a-din	עדין
Worker for the community				as-kan	עסקן
Public	tsi-bu-rit	ציבורית	הציבורי	tsi-bu-ri	ציבורי
Modest	tse-nu-a	צנועה	הצנוע	tse-nu-a	צנוע
Saintly	tsad-ka-nit	צדקנית	הצדיק	tse-dek	צדק
Happy	se-mei-cha	שמחה		sa-mei-ach	שמח
Simple, modest or perfect	te-mi-mah	תמימה		tam or ta-mim	תמים or תם

Passive voice format:

In the previous section, an example of the active voice syntax was "Our beloved Father," אבינו היקר. This section describes the passive voice format, as with "He was beloved to his children", יקר לבניו.

The general syntax is as follows:
  a. < He/She was "adjective">
  b. <to, in, by, among>
  c. <his/her "one or more relationships or nouns">

Examples: Passive Voice Format

| 1. He was faithful to his wife | Ne-e-man le-ish-to | נאמן לאשתו |
| 2. She was beloved to her children | Ye-ka-ra le-va-ne-ha | יקרה לבניה |

a. The adjectives may be strung together with the prefix letter ו meaning "and." For example: "He was faithful to his wife, and beloved to his children and to his people." נאמן לאשתו וַיקר לבניו וַלעמו. (Note that the "vavs" linking the parts of the phrase are underlined for clarity.) "The pronouns of "he/she," as well as the verb "was" are implied.

The vocabulary list of adjectives for the "Passive Voice Format" is the same as presented earlier in this chapter for the "Active Voice Format."

b. "To" or "by" are represented by "ל". "In" or "among" are represented by "ב." For example:

| 1. He was beloved to his children | Ya-kar le-va-nav | יקר לַבניו |
| 2. He was respected in the comunity | Ki-bud ba-ka-hal | כבוד בַקהל |

66

c. A noun describing the deceased's relationship to the living follows one of the above mentioned letters.

Most of the nouns in the list that follows have a pronominal ending. The list is alphabetical by the second letter of the Hebrew word in the right column or the first letter of the word following the Hebrew preposition, "בָ" or "לְ" discussed above. For that reason, the second letter is underlined as in the example בָאָדָם, where the prefix for the noun, "adam, אָדָם", is the "ba, בָ" meaning "among." Masculine forms are presented first, followed by feminine forms.

Nouns with associated prefix in the "Passive voice format"

<u>Male</u>

English	Transliteration	Hebrew
Among men	ba-a-dam	בָּאָדָם
To his wife	le-ish-to	לְאִשְׁתּוֹ
To his son	li-ve-no	לִבְנוֹ
To his sons (children)	le-va-nav	לְבָנָיו
To his daughters	li-ve-no-tav	לִבְנוֹתָיו
To his daughter	le-vi-to	לְבִתּוֹ
To his friends	le-cha-vei-rav	לַחֲבֵרָיו
To his orphans (or mourners)	le-ya-to-mav	לִיתוֹמָיו
To his family	le-mish-pa-cha-to	לְמִשְׁפַּחְתּוֹ
To his grandchildren	le-nech-dav	לְנֶכְדָּיו
To his community	le-ei-da-to	לַעֲדָתוֹ
In his community	le-ei-da-to	בַּעֲדָתוֹ
To his people	le-a-mo	לְעַמּוֹ
Among his people	ba-a-mo	בְּעַמּוֹ
In the community	ba-ka-hal	בַּקָּהָל
To his students	le-tal-mi-dav	לְתַלְמִידָיו

67

<u>Female</u>

To her son	li-ve-na	לִבְנָהּ
To her sons	le-va-ne-ha	לְבָנֶיהָ
To her daughters	li-ve-no-ta	לִבְנוֹתֶהָ
To her husband	le-va-a-la	לְבַעְלָהּ
To her daughter	le-vi-ta	לְבִתָּהּ
To her friends	le-cha-vei-ro-te-ha	לְחַבְרוֹתֶיהָ
To her orphans (or mourners)	le-ya-to-me-ha	לִיתוֹמֶיהָ
To her family	le-mish-pa-cha-ta	לְמִשְׁפַּחְתָּהּ
To her grandchildren	le-nech-de-ha	לְנֶכְדֶּיהָ
In her community	ba-ei-da-ta	בַּעֲדָתָהּ
To her community	le-ei-da-ta	לַעֲדָתָהּ
Among her people	ba-a-ma	בְּעַמָּהּ
To her people	le-a-ma	לְעַמָּהּ
To her students	le-tal-mi-de-ha	לְתַלְמִידֶיהָ

Format Descriptive of the Deceased

This format often overlaps with the epitaph section. Instead of describing the individual with respect to survivors, this format describes the individuals with respect to his/her personal characteristics or the thing(s) he/she did in his/her lifetime. The list of common descriptive nouns follows. For the adjectives, refer back to the list presented earlier in this chapter.

The syntax is as follows. In many cases, the noun is prefixed by "the, ה" which is shown parenthetically in the list.

      a.   b.

<noun or profession><one or more adjectives>
Examples:

A man of integrity and uprightness	Ish tam ve-yashar	אִישׁ תָּם וְיָשָׁר
A proper woman	I-sha ke-sha-ra	אִשָּׁה כְּשֵׁרָה

68

Nouns describing the deceased

Young man (married)	av-reich	[ה]אברך
Man	ish	[ה]איש
Woman	i-shah	[ה]אשה
Young man	ba-chur	[ה]בחור
Young woman	ba-chu-ra	[ה]בחורה
Son	ben	[ה]בן
Daughter	bat	[ה]בת
Friend (masc.)	cha-ver	חבר
Friend (fem.)	cha-vei-ra	חברה
Son-in-law or young man	cha-tan	[ה]חתן
A Jew (masc.)	ye-hu-di	יהודי
A Jew (fem.)	ye-hu-dit	יהודית
Boy	ye-led	[ה]ילד
Girl	ya-le-da	[ה]ילדה
Literally: bride. Usage: young woman	ka-lah	[ה]כלה
Young man	na-ar	[ה]נער
Young woman	na-a-ra	[ה]נערה
Young man	e-lem	[ה]עלם
Young woman	a-le-ma	[ה]עלמה
Grandfather	sa-bah	סבא
Grandmother	sab-tah	סבתא

Professions of the deceased:

Torah reader	ba-al ko-rei	בעל קורא	ב"ק
Sounder of the Ram's horn	ba-al to-kah	בעל תוקע	ב"ת
Sounder of the Ram's horn	ba-al te-ki-ah	בעל תקיעה	ב"ת
Cantor	cha-zan	חזן	
Story teller, preacher	ma-gid	מגיד	
Teacher	mo-reh (mo-rah)	מורה	

69

Scribe	so-fer	סופר	
Scribe of Torah -Tephillen, Mezzuzot		סופר תורה־תפלין מזוזות	סת"ם
Rabbi	ha-rav	הרב	הר'
Doctor	ro-fei	רופא	
Ritual slaughterer	sho-chet u-ve-dok	שוחט ובדוק	שו"ב
Prayer leader	she-li-ach tsi-bur	שליח צבור	ש"ץ

Introductory Statement about a Monument

Sometimes the first Hebrew line states that you are looking at a monument. The following list includes the most common examples:

A stone of tears	e-ven ba-chot	אבן בכות
Monument	gil-ad	גלעד
For perpetual memory	le-maz-ke-ret nei-tsach	למזכרת נצח
Monument	ma-tsei-va	מצבה
Monument of memorial	ma-tsei-vat zi-ka-ron	מצבת זכרון
Monument (literally: Soul)	ne-fesh	נפש
Monument	tsi-yun	ציון

Sometimes the introductory statement about the monument leads naturally into other types of the "First Hebrew Line" or the deceased's name (represented as "..."):

| A stone of darkness and death to... | e-ven a-fal... ve-tsal-ma-vet... | אבן אפל וצלמות... |

| Praise be the Righteous Judge | Ba-ruch da-yan ha-e-met | ברוך דיין האמת | בד"ה |

(A blessing offered acknowledging and accepting God's will.)

| Place of | ma-kom | מ״ק ...   מקום קבר ... |
| the grave of ... | ke-ver ... | |

A valley of groans	ei-mek ha-ya-gon	עמק היגון
a stone of tears	e-ven ba-chot	אבן בכות
to the memory of ...	le-zich-ron ...	לזכרון ...

A monument	tsi-yun	ציון אבל כבד
of intense mourning	a-val ka-veid	
to the young man ...	le-av-reaich ...	לאברך ...

| A monument | tsi-yun ... | ציון לנפש חיה ... |
| to a living soul ... | le-ne-fesh cha-ya | |

| A monument to | tsi-yun | ציון לנפש יקרה ... |
| a beloved soul ... | le-ne-fesh ye-ka-ra ... | |

| A voice of tears | Kol be-chi (ne-hi) | קול בכי (נהי) |

The following examples (both from Chevra Kadisha of Chelsea, Woburn, MA) combine many of the above phrases and ideas:

Example #1

This stone was	Ha-e-ven ha-zot	האבן הזאת הוקמה פה
established here	huk-ma po	
as a tombstone	le-ma-tsei-va	למצבה ולציון
and monument	u-le-tsi-yon	
for under this	ki ta-chat ha-gal ...	כי תחת הגל ...
mound is ...		

Example #2

This stone will be	Ha-e-ven ha-zot ti-yeh	האבן הזאת תהיה
a monument and	le-ma-tsei-va	למצבה ולאלון בכות
a tree of tears	u-le-ei-lon ba-chot	
and a monument...	u-le-tsi-yun...	ולציון לנפש ...
to a soul...	le-ne-fesh...	

Place, Organization or City of Origin

Sometimes there will be a line indicating organizational membership, city/place of origin.

Synagogue affiliation is often introduced by the abbreviation ק"ק meaning קהלה קדושה (ke-hi-lat ke-du-sha) which translates to "Holy Congregation" followed by the name of the temple.

The place of origin of the deceased is often introduced by the letter "מ", meaning "from." If a city name follows, the name of the city may be proceeded by מעיר or abbreviated מע' (mei-ir) which translates to "from the city of."

If the city happens to be an historically "holy city", such as Jerusalem, Tsefat (Safad), Hebron, etc., the city name may be preceeded by ... מעיר הקדוש or abbreviated מעה"ק (mei-ir ha-ko-desh) which translates to "from the holy city of..."

72

6. Name Line

Decoration:	פ ☆ נ
Introductory Line:	אבינו היקר
Name Line:	יצחק בן יוסף
Dateline:	נפ" כ"ח ניסן תשל"ז
	Isaac Stone
	Died April 16, 1977
Epitaph:	תנ'צ'ב'ה'

As newer generations come from increasingly assimilated backgrounds, Hebrew is used less on monuments. However, if there is any Hebrew on a monument, it is usually the deceased's name.

The most common name syntax as shown in Chapter 3, "Monuments 101" is:

Here lies <title><name of deceased><son/daughter of> <title> <parent's name> <last name>

The following format is a slightly expanded version of the "name line," which offers a few additional possibilities:

   1.   2a.   2b.   2c.   3.   2a.   2b.
Here lies <title><name of deceased><descriptor><son/daughter of> <title><father's name>

       2c.   4. 2a.   2b.   2c.   5.
<descriptor> and <title><mother's name><descriptor><last name>

An unusual variant is when the mother's name precedes the father's name, or when only the mother's name is used. In Israeli military cemeteries, where the deceased was a war casualty, only the mother's name is used. In most of these cases, the deceased's life was cut off prematurely. Since mothers are usually the more nurturing parent, using the mother's name only or the mother's name first, would invoke the feminine, more nurturing characteristics of God when the name of the deceased is mentioned.

Note that the name does not always start at the beginning of a line. If it is not clear where the name starts, look for 1. (Here lies), 2a. (title) or 3. (son/daughter of). At least one of these elements will be recognizable.

1. Here lies

In Chapter 5, there was only one option suggested for "here lies" (namely: פ"נ). The following additional options cover the possibilities for more than 95% of all monuments.

Po nik-bar (masc.)	פה נקבר	פ"נ
Po nik-be-ra (fem.)	פה נקברה	פ"נ
nik-bar po (masc.)	נקבר פה	נ"פ
nik-be-ra po (fem.)	נקברה פה	נ"פ
Po nit-man (masc.)	פה נטמן	פ"נ
Po nit-ma-na (fem.)	פה נטמנה	פ"נ
Po ta-mun (masc.)	פה טמון	פ"ט
Po te-mu-na (fem.)	פה טמונה	פ"ט
In Yiddish:	A-heir resht	אהער רעשט
	Da ligt	דא ליגט
	Da roit	דא רוהט
In Ladino:	A-ki rei-po-za	אקי ריפוזה

"Here lies" is sometimes omitted in the "Name Line" if it was already included in the decoration at the top of the stone (Chapter 4) or at the beginning of the "Introductory Hebrew Line" (Chapter 5).

Less common options include:
In this place Ba-ma-kom ha-zeh במקום הזה ב"ה

74

This acronym could mean any of the following: נל"ע

Departed for his eternal home. נפטר לבית עולמו
    [i.e euphemism for "the grave"]
Departed for her eternal home. נפטרה לבית עולמה
Departed for paradise. נפטר(ה) לגן עדן
Departed for eternal life. נפטר(ה) לחיי עד
    [i.e euphemism for "death"]

Here rests	Po me-na-veh (me-na-va)	פה מנוה	פ"מ
Here rests	Po ma-nu-ach (masc.)	פה מנוח	פ"מ
Here rests	Po me-nu-cha (fem.)	פה מנוחה	פ"מ
Here lies	Po nik-bar	פה נקבר גוית...	
the body of...	gi-vi-yat... (masc.)		
Here lies	Po nik-be-ra	פה נקברה גוית...	
the body of...	gi-vi-yat... (fem.)		
To remember	Liz-kor nish-mat...	לזכר נשמת...	
the soul of...			

2. Name syntax or format (2a., 2b., and 2c.)

The same syntax for the name of the deceased is repeated for the name of the father and mother of the deceased. That format is as follows:

    a.   **b.**   **c.**
<Title><name(s)><Descriptor>

a. Titles:
The following list is representative of the "titles" one may find at the beginning of the name. Often no title is used.

The young man (married)	Ha-av-reich	האברך	
The man	Ha-ish	האיש	ה'
The woman	Ha-i-sha	האשה	ה'
The young man	Ha-ba-chur	הבחור	הבח'
(over 13 but unmarried)			

English	Transliteration	Hebrew	Abbrev.
The young woman (over 13 but unmarried)	Ha-ba-chu-rah	הבחורה	הבח'
The young woman (literally: virgin)	Ha-be-tu-la	הבתולה	
Mr. (The man)	Ha-ga-vir	הגביר	
The boy (usually under age 13)	Ha-ye-led	הילד	
The girl (usually under age 13)	Ha-ye-le-da	הילדה	
The honored sir.	Ha-a-don ha-nech-bad	האדון הנכבד	ה'ה'

Note: The abbreviation, ה'ה', offers the possibility of any noun/adjective combination. There are many other possibilities.

English	Transliteration	Hebrew	Abbrev.
The honored sir	Ke-vod ha-a-don	כבוד האדון	כ'ה'
The honored rabbi	Ke-vod ha-rav	כבוד הרב	כ'ה'
The honored ...	Ke-vod ...	כבוד...	כ'...
Mr.	Mar	מר	מ'
Mrs./Miss	Ma-rat	מרת	מ' or מר'
The young man	Ha-e-lem	העלם	
The young woman	Ha-al-ma	העלמה	
The modest one	Ha-tse-nu-ah	הצנועה	הצנ' or הצ'
Mister	Reb	רב	ר'
Rabbi	Ha-rav	הרב	

Less common titles:

English	Transliteration	Hebrew
Master (also, General)	Ha-a-luf	האלוף
Genius	Ha-ga-on	הגאון
Synagogue leader	Ha-ga-bai	הגבאי
Judge	Ha-da-yan	הדיין or הדין

Teacher	Ha-me-la-med	המלמד
The late	Ha-ma-nu-ach (cha)	(ה)המנוח
The saintly one (masc.)	Ha-tsa-dik	הצדיק
The saintly one (fem.)	Ha-tsa-di-ka-nit	הצדיקנית
Synagogue leader	Ha-ke-tsin	הקצין
Community leader	Ha-Rosh	הראש
Daughter or wife of a rabbi	Ha-Ra-ba-nit	הרבנית
The physician	Ha-Ro-fei	הרופא
Synagogue caretaker	Ha-Sha-mash	השמש

Additional Superlatives:

Sometimes additional superlatives are inserted into the deceased's title, which reflect the relationship of the community to the deceased.

My master, my teacher & my rabbi	A-do-ni mo-ri ve-ra-bi	אדמו"ר אדוני מורי ורבי
Our master, our teacher, & our rabbi	A-do-nei-nu mo-rei-nu ve-ra-bei-nu	אדמו"ר אדוננו מורנו ורבנו
The sainted Rabbi	Ha-rav	הרה"צ הרב הצדיק

b. Name

The individual name of the deceased may take any of the following formats, listed in decreasing order of frequency:

> First name
> First name, Middle name
> First name, Last name
> First name, Middle name, Last name

Frequency of Names

Usually, the same 50 men's names and an equal number of women's names make up 85% of the names that appear on monuments[11]. Of course, names come in and out of popularity. The names listed below typically represent those of Jews born between 1850 and 1950 who are Ashkenazi, descended from the European Jews whose names were often Yiddish. See Chapter 2 for more information on Yiddish names and Yiddish vocalization. With the emergence of Hebrew in the twentieth century, many young rabbis are discouraging parents from using the Yiddish names. So it can be anticipated that in another century, the mixture of names will change radically. That said, many of the Hebrew Biblical names have been timeless and have remained popular throughout the ages.

Spelling Problems

Hebrew names tend to be Biblical and follow Biblical spellings. However, the problem of misspellings and multiple spellings for the same name occurs even in the Bible. Two examples follow:

English	Spelling #1	Spelling #2
David	דוד	דויד
Jesse	ישי	אישי

However, in Yiddish, there are no Biblical standards and spellings varied with local accents. I cite two extreme examples:

The woman's name, nominally pronounced in English as Reizel, contains three consonants and two vowels. All of the following permutations of spellings appear on monuments:

---

[11] The methodology for determining this list was as follows:
Approximately 150 monuments were examined from each of 10 different cemeteries. Each name that appeared was tabulated. Men's monuments provided an average of three men's names: one or two for the man and one or two for the man's father. Women's monuments provided an average of 1.5 women's names for the deceased and an average of 1.5 men's names of the deceased's father. In family plots where it was obvious that multiple generations of the same family were buried, the duplicate names were not counted twice.

R	ר			
ei	י	יי	רי	Nothing
z	ז	צ		
e	י	ע	א	Nothing
l	ל			

The man's name, nominally pronounced in English as Velvel, contains four consonants and two vowels. All of the following permutations of spellings appear.

V	ו	וו		
e	י	ע	א	
l	ל			
v	ו	וו	ב	
e	י	ע	א	Nothing
l	ל			

Names such as Dinah which end in a short "a" sound are sometimes spelled with the Yiddish ending, "aleph" or "ayin," or the Hebrew ending, "hei."

Male/Female Differences

The percentage of Yiddish Women's names is far higher than men's names. One reason is that more than 90% of the names in the Bible are men's names. Therefore, women have fewer choices from in the Bible.

In addition, a number of men's names often come in a Hebrew/Yiddish pairing. The Hebrew name is first when the two are together. There is no equivalent among women's names. The following are the most common of these:

Men's Names

Yiddish	Translit.	Hebrew Equivalent	Translit.	English Equiv.	Most Common Meaning
אייזק	Isaac	יצחק	Yits-chak	Isaac	Laughter
בער	Ber	דב	Dov	Barney /Bernard	Bear
הערש or הירש	Hirsh or Hersch	צבי	Tsvi	Harry	Deer
העשיל	Heschel	יהושע	Ye-ho-shu-a	Joshua	God will save
וועלוויל	Velvel	זאב	Ze-eiv	William or Bill	Wolf
וואלף	Wolf	זאב	Ze-eiv	Wolf	Wolf
לייב	Leib	יהודה	Ye-hu-dah	Judah or Louis	Lion
לייב	Leib	אריה	Ar-yei	Louis	Lion
מענדיל	Mendel	מנחם	Me-na-chem	Max	Comfort
נטע	Na-ta	נתן	Na-tan	Nathan	Gift
פייבש	Fi-vish	שרגא (Aramaic)	Shraga	Phillip	Bright one

Diminutives

In English, we frequently turn a name into a diminutive as follows: Richard becomes Richie; Elizabeth becomes Lizzie.

Yiddish diminutives can occur on monuments by using the "k" sound.

Example:

English	Hebrew	Yiddish	Yiddish Translit.	Yiddish Diminutive	Yiddish Dimin. Translit.
Isaiah	ישעיה	שיעה	Shi-ya	שיקע	She-keh
Chai-ya	חיה	חיה	Chai-ya	חייקע	Chai-keh

The second method of making diminutives is by adding a "la-med" to the end.

A third method of making diminutives is by adding an "a" to the end of the name. The examples below give both diminutives for the same name.

Example:

Yiddish	Yiddish Translit.	First Yiddish Dimin.	Yiddish Dimin. Translit.	Second Yiddish Dimin.	Yiddish Dimin. Translit.
לייב	Leib	לייבל	Lei-bel	לייבלע	Lei-be-la
רייזע	Rei-za	רייזעל	Rei-zel	רייזעלע	Rei-ze-la

List of names:

The two lists that follow are the 50 most popular men's names and the 50 most popular women's names that represent about 85% of the Hebrew/Yiddish names on monument inscriptions. They are listed alphabetically by the Hebrew. Diminutives are not counted separately. Variant spellings are added parenthetically. There are thousands of names and since there are several good resources for Yiddish and Hebrew names[12], this book will not duplicate their efforts. Note that there are cases where there is no correlation between the Hebrew name and the English name on a monument.

---

[12] Kolatch, A. J., *The New Name Dictionary* (Jonathan David, NY, 1989)

The 50 Most Common Men's Names

English	Derivation	Transliteration	Hebrew
Aba	Hebrew: Father	A-ba	אבא
Abraham	Biblical	Av-ra-ham	אברהם
Aaron	Biblical	A-ha-ron	אהרן
Isaac	Yiddish: Isaac	I-sak	אייזיק
Elijah	Biblical	Ei-li-ya-hu	אליהו
Eliezer	Biblical	E-li-e-zer	אליעזר
Ephraim	Biblical	Ef-ra-yim	אפרים
Aryeh (Ari)	Hebrew: Lion	Ar-yei (A-ri)	אריה (ארי)
Asher	Biblical	A-sher	אשר
Ben Zion	Hebrew: Son of Zion	Ben Tsi-yon	בן ציון
Benjamin	Biblical	Bin-ya-min	בנימין
Bear	Yiddish: Bear	Bear	בער
Baruch	Hebrew: Blessing	Ba-ruch	ברוך
Gershon	Biblical	Ger-shon	גרשון
Dov	Hebrew: Bear	Dov	דוב (דאב)
David	Biblical	Da-vid	דוד
Hirsch	Yiddish: Deer	Hirsch	הירש (הערש)
Wolf (William)	Yiddish: Wolf	Wolf	וואלף (ווילף)
Wolf (William)	Hebrew: Wolf	Ze-eiv	זאב
Zelman	Yiddish: Variant of Solomon	Zel-man	זלמן
Zelig	Transliterated from vernacular	Ze-lig	זעליג
Chaim (Hyman)	Hebrew: Life	Cha-yim	חיים
Tuviah	Hebrew: God is good	Tu-vi-ya	טוביה
Judah	Biblical	Ye-hu-da	יהודה
Joshua	Biblical	Ye-ho-shu-a	יהושע
Joseph	Biblical	Yo-seiph	יוסף
Ezekiel	Biblical	Ye-chez-keil	יחזקאל
Jehiel	Biblical	Ye-chi-eil	יחיאל (יכיאל)

Jacob	Biblical	Ya-a-kov	יעקב
Isaac	Biblical	Yits-chak	יצחק
Isaiah	Biblical	Ye-shi-ya (Ye-shi-ya-hu)	ישעיה(ו)
Israel	Biblical	Yis-ra-eil	ישראל
Leib	Yiddish: Lion	Leib	לייב (ליב)
Meyer	Hebrew: One who shines	Mei-ir	מאיר
Michael	Biblical	Mi-cha-eil (Mi-chel)	מיכאל (מיכל)
Menahem	Biblical	Me-na-chem	מנחם
Mendel	Yiddish: Menahem	Men-del	מענדל (מענדיל)
Mordecai	Biblical	Mor-de-cai	מרדכי
Moses	Biblical	Mo-she	משה
Nachum	Biblical	Na-chum	נחום
Neta	Yiddish: Nathan	Ne-ta	נטע (נאטע)
Nathan	Biblical	Na-tan	נתן
Phineas	Biblical	Pin-chas	פנחס
Pesach	Hebrew: Pasover	Pe-sach	פסח
Tsvi	Hebrew: Deer	Tse-vi	צבי
Reuben	Biblical	Re-u-vein	ראובן
Shalom	Hebrew: Peace	Sha-lom	שלום
Solomon	Biblical	She-lo-mo	שלמה
Samuel	Biblical	She-mu-eil	שמואל
Simcha	Hebrew: Joy	Sim-cha	שמחה

The 50 Most Common Women's Names

English	Derivation	Transliteration	Hebrew
Etta	Transliterated from vernacular	E-ta	אטא (איטא, איטע, עטע...)
Esther	Biblical	Es-ter	אסתר
Belle	Yiddish: Bilhah (Biblical)	Bei-leh	ביילה (ביילע)
Blooma	Transliterated from vernacular	Blu-ma	בלומה (בלומע)
Brina	Yiddish: Brunette	Bri-na	ברינה (brיינע)
Beracha	Hebrew: Blessing	Be-ra-cha	ברכה
Basha	Hebrew: Daughter of God	Bat-ya	בתיה
	Yiddish variant spellings	Ba-sha	באסיה (באשע)
Bathsheba (Sheba	Biblical:	Bat She-va or She-va	בת שבע (שבע)
Golda	Transliterated from vernacular	Gol-da	גאלדא (גאלדע)
Gittel	Yiddish: Good	Gi-tel	גיטל (גיטאל, גיטעל)
Deborah	Biblical	De-vo-ra	דבורה
Dinah	Biblical	Di-na	דינה (דינע)
Hinda	Yiddish: Deer		הינדא (הינדע)
Henna	Yiddish.: Variant of Hannah	He-neh	הינה (העננ, העננא, היעננ)
Zisa, Sisel	Yiddish: sweet	Zi-sa	זיסא (זיסע)
	Yiddish variant spellings	Zi-sel (Zis-la)	זיסל (זיסלא)
Zelda	Transliterated from vernacular	Zel-da	זעלדה (זעלדע)
Chasya	Yiddish: protected by God	Chas-ya	חאסיע (חאשא, חסיה)
Eve	Biblical	Cha-va	חוה

Chaya	Biblical	Cha-ya	חיה
Hannah	Biblical	Cha-na	חנה
	Yiddish variant spellings		חינע (חיענע)
Tobie	Hebrew: Good	To-vah	טובה
	Yiddish variant spelling		טובא (טובע)
Judith	Biblical	Ye-hu-dit	יהודית
Jetta	Yid.: Var. of Judith	Ye-ta	ייטע (יטא, יעטא)
Leah	Biblical	Lei-ah	לאה
Libby	Yiddish: Loved one	Li-ba	ליבא (ליבע)
Minnie	Yid: Var. of Miriam	Mi-na	מינא
			(מינע, מאניע, מיניה)
	Diminutive: Min-del		מינדיל (מינדל, מינדעל)
Mollie	Biblical	Mal-kah	מלכה
Miriam	Biblical	Mir-yam	מרים
Nechama	Feminine of Biblical:	Ne-cha-ma	נחמה
	Na-chum		
	Yiddish variant spelling	Na-cha	נעחא (נעחע, נעכע)
Sasha, Sissy	Transliterated		סאסיע
	from vernacular		(סאשה, שאסיע, שאשא)
Ethel	Transliterated	E-tel	עטיל
	from vernacular		(עטל, אטיל)
Elka	Transliterated	El-ka	עלקא
	from vernacular		(עלקע, עלכע)
Fay	Yiddish: Bird	Fei-geh	פייגה
			(פייגע, פיגא...)
	Diminutive	Fei-gel	פייגל (פייגעל)
Pesha	Yid.: Var. of Basha	Pe-si	פעסי
			(פעשה, פעסיע, פסיה...)
Pearl	Transliterated	Pe-ril	פעריל
	from vernacular		
Freida	Yiddish: Peace	Frei-da	פריידא (פריידע)
	Diminutive: Frei-del		פריידל (פראדל, פרידעל)

Name	Meaning	Pronunciation	Hebrew
Fruma	Yiddish: Ritually observant	Fru-ma	פרומא (פרומע)
Tsiv-ya	Hebrew: Doe	Tsiv-ya	צביה
Tsipa	Hebrew: Hope	Tsi-pa	ציפא (ציפה)
Tsira	Yiddish: Var. of Sarah	Tsi-ra	צירע
	Diminutive	Tsi-ril	צירל
Rocha, Rochelle	Yid.: Var. of Rachel	Rosha	ראשא
			(רעשא, רעשאל, רישא, ריסע)
Rebecca	Biblical	Riv-kah	רבקה
Rachel	Biblical	Ra-cheil	רחל
Reba	Yiddish: Rebecca	Ri-ba	ריבא (ריבע)
Rose, Risa, etc.	Yiddish: God is my secret	Rei-sa	ריזא
			(רויזע, רייצע)
Rosie	Yiddish: Diminutive of Rei-sa	Rei-zel	רייזל (רייזל,
			רייזעלע, רייצעל, רייזיל, ריסע...)
Rina	Hebrew/Yiddish: Joy	Ri-na	רנה (ריינא, ראנע)
Shana	Yiddish: Beautiful	Sha-na	שיינא (שיינה)
	Yiddish: Diminutive of Shana	Shen-del	שיינדיל
Shifra	Biblical	Shi-fra	שפרה
Sarah	Biblical	Sa-rah	שרה

c. Descriptor:

Jews became associated with tribes, originally corresponding to the twelve sons of Jacob (Exodus 1:2ff, inter alia). A descendant of any tribe but Levi is known as an Israelite. The designation of "Israelite" on a monument is unusual. Descendants of the tribe of Levi are further divided into Priests (Kohanim) and Levites. The designation of "Priest" or "Levite" often appears on monuments.

The options for tribal descriptors are as follows:

The Priest	Ha-Ko-hein	הכהן	
The Righteous Priest	Katz (Ko-hein tsa-dik)	כהן צדיק	כ״ץ
The Levite	Ha-Lei-vi	הלוי or הלוי	
The Levite	Segal (Se-gan la-ke-hu-na) Literally: Assistant to the priesthood	סגן לכהונה	סג״ל
The Israelite	Ha-Yis-ra-eil	הישראל	

Sometimes one of the following abbreviations follows the name in addition to or in lieu of the above descriptors.

May his(her) Memory be a blessing	zich-ro-no (zich-ro-na) li-ve-ra-cha	זכרונו (זכרונה) לברכה	ז״ל
May the memory of the righteous be a blessing	Zei-cher tsa-dik li-ve-ra-cha	זכר צדיק לברכה	ז׳צ׳ל
May his light shine	nei-ro ya-ir	נרו יאיר	נ״י
May his(her) rest be Eden	nu-cho (nu-cha) ei-din	נוחו (נוחה) עדן	נ״ע
Rest in Peace	A-lav(A-le-ha). ha-sha-lom	עליו (עליה) השלום	ע״ה

Very occasionally, Sephardic elitism is shown by the addition of the following to the end of a name:

Pure Sephardic (Spaniard)	Se-far-di Ta-hor	ספרדי טהור	ס״ט

3. Relationships

This entry is straightforward and requires little or no explanation.

Son of	Ben	בן
Son of Mister ...	Ben reb (Bar)	בר" בן רב
Also: Daughter of Mister	Bat reb (Bar)	בר" בת רב
Daughter of	Bat	בת
Daughter of Mrs.	Bat ma-rat	בת מ' בת מרת
Of the family of	Di	(Ladino) די

If the person was a convert to Judaism the Father's name may be given as:

Abraham our father	Av-ra-ham	אברהם	א'א'
	a-vi-nu	אבינו	

Very few older monuments provide the name of the deceased's mother. This is changing in the newer cemeteries associated with the more liberal movements of Judaism.

4. and

The letter "*vav*" (ו), pronounced "ve" or "u" is appended to second parent's name, when both names appear on the monument.

Example:

Samuel son of	She-mu-eil ben	שמואל בן
Solomon	she-lo-mo	שלמה
and Miriam	u-Mir-yam	ומרים

5. Last name/Family Name

Last names sometimes appear at the end of the "name line." However, if the last name is included, it usually appears on a line by itself below the "name line." Most monuments that include the family name in Hebrew often also include it in the vernacular. So, it is usually easy to recognize the last name based the consonants. Most of the time, transliterations use Yiddish vocalization methods. See chapter 2 for pronunciation rules for Yiddish.

A few examples follow:

Fishman	פישמאַן
Gottfried	גאַטפריד
Nightingale	נייטינגייל
Reingold	רייַנגאָלד
Schwartz	שוואַרץ

7. The Date Line

Decoration:	פ ✡ נ
Introductory Line:	אבינו היקר
Name Line:	יצחק בן יוסף
Dateline:	נפ" כ"ח ניסן תשל"ז
	Isaac Stone
	Died April 16, 1977
Epitaph:	תנ'צ'ב'ה'

The most common format of the date line is the format described in Chapter 3, "Monuments 101". It is as follows:

Died <day><month><year>   <year><month><day> "נפ

Specific example:

Died 28 Nisan 5737   נפ" כ"ח ניסן תשל"ז

There are many variants that occur in increasing levels of complexity. The format referred to below as <date>, is either "<day><month>" or a holiday.

```
  A.        C.        E.     D.
Born <day of the week><date><year>

  B.        C.        E.     D.
Died <day of the week><date><year>


          F.
<Age of the deceased>
```

A. Born

The date of birth is rarely given in Hebrew. When it is, it is introduced as:

Born (masc.)	ha-yu-lad	הַיוּלד
Born (fem.)	ha-yu-le-det	הַיוּלדת
Born (masc.)	no-lad	נוֹלד
Born (fem.)	no-le-da	נוֹלדה
Born (Yiddish)	Ge-boi-ren	געבוירען

B. Died

Chapter 3 offered only "נפ" to indicate that the person died. The several other options presented below cover more than 95% of monuments.

| Died | Nif-tar (Nif-te-ra) | נפ" or נ'   נפטר(ה) |
| Died | Na-fal | נפל |

In military cemeteries (especially in Israel), na-fal, meaning "fell," implies "fell in battle".

While the vast majority of monuments use *nif-tar* (נפטר) to indicate that the person died, what follows is a list of 38 other euphemisms and synonyms for death.

| Blessed are you in your departure.(Deut. 28:6) | Ba-ruch a-ta be-tsei-te-cha | ברוך אתה בצאתך |

| He (she) came to his (her) rest. | Ba(-ah) li-me-nu-cha-to (li-me-nu-cha-ta) | בא(ה) למנוחתו (למנוחתה) |

| In the days of his (her) youth | Bi-mei a-li-mu-to (a-li-mu-ta) | בימי עלימותו (עלימותה) |

| She died an untimely death | be-o-da be-i-ba ka-te-fa ha-ma-vet | בעודה באבה קטפה המות |

92

Died	Ga-va	גוע (גועה)
Died (Yiddish)	Gesh-tar-ben	געשטרבען
His time arrived to see life	hi-gi-a to-ro lir-ot cha-yim	הגיע תורו לראות חיים
He passed away (She passed away)	Ha-lach le-o-la-mo (Ha-le-cha le-o-la-ma)	הלך לעולמו (הלכה לעולמה)
Transferred to the heights	Huk-na ma-rom	הוקנה מרום
His (her) soul departed to dwell in the heights	Ha-le-cha nish-ma-to(ta) lish-kon ba-me-ro-mim	הלכה נשמתו(ה) לשכון במרומים
Who was taken. from us	Ha-nil-kach (Ha-nil-ke-cha) mei-i-ta-nu	הנלקח(ה) מאתנו
The day of death of ... was	Yom pe-ti-rat ...	יום פטירת ...
His soul departed in purity	Ya-tsa nish-ma-to ba-ta-ha-ra	ינ"ב (יצאה נשמתו בטהרה)
Descended to the grave	Ya-rad (ya-re-da) ba-ke-ver	ירד(ה) בקבר
Died	Meit (Mei-ta)	מת (מתה)
Gathered to his. (her) people (i.e. Died)	Ne-e-saf el a-mo (ne-e-se-fa el a-me-ha)	נאסף אל עמו (נאספה אל עמה)

cut off in his prime	nig-da be-i-bo	נגדע באבו
Was cut off...	Nig-zar (nig-ze-ra)	נגזר(נגזרה)
Was cut off from the land of the living.	Nig-zar(nig-ze-ra) mei-e-rets ha-cha-yim.	נגזר(נגזרה) מארץ החיים
Departed to the heights of heaven,	Nis-ta-leik li-she-mei ma-rom	נסתלק לשמי מרום
Taken (died) suddenly	Nik-taf (nik-te-fa) pit-om	נקטף (נקטפה) פתאום
Taken (died) from the land of the living.	Nik-taf (nik-te-fa) mei-e-rets ha-cha-yim.	נקטף (נקטפה) מארץ החיים
His (Her) light was extinguished	Nei-ro (Nei-ra) Ka-vah	נרו (נרה) כבה
He (She) left us	A-zav(A-ze-va) o-ta-nu	עזב(ה) אותנו
He (She) left the land of the living	A-zav(A-ze-va) e-rets ha-cha-yim	עזב(ה) ארץ החיים
He (She) departed life	A-zav(A-ze-va) et ha-cha-yim	עזב(ה) את החיים
He departed his world (She departed her world	A-zav chal-do A-ze-va chal-da	עזב חלדו (עזבה חלדה
Concerning the death of...	al pe-ti-rat	(ע"פ) על פטירת
A flower cut off	Pe-rach ka-tuf (on a child's grave)	פרח קטוף

Suddenly …	pit-om …	...פתאום

(usually followed immediately by any of the many ways of saying, "he/she died.")

Suddenly the end. came upon him	pit-om ba a-lav ha-ke-rets	פתאום בא עליו הקרץ
The grave took him in his youth	ke-ver hu-val be-i-ba-ho	קבר הובל באבהו
Death took him.	ka-te-fa-hu ha-ma-vet	קטפהו המות
Returned to the dirt	shav le-ad-ma-to (ta)(ה)	שב לאדמתו(ה)
Departed from life (Literally: Abandoned life for all life)	Sha-vak cha-yim le-kol chai	שבק חיים לכל חי (שחל"ח)
Who went to his world (Who went to her world	She-ha-lach le-o-la-mo She-ha-le-cha le-o-la-ma	שהלך לעולמו (שהלכה לעולמה)
Who was taken before his time Who was taken before her time	She-nik-taf be-lo i-to She-nik-te-fa be-lo i-ta	שנקטף בלא עתו שנקטפה בלא עתה
The glory of ... has Departed	Sha-ka shim-sho shel ...	שקעה שמשו של ...

C. Day of the Week

Sometimes, the day of the week on which the person died is included on the date line. The following table lists the Hebrew names for days of the week.

95

There is an ambiguity between the day of the week and the day of the month that is shown later in this chapter. The example of this ambiguity appears after the explanation of the day of the month.

Table of Days of the Week

English	Transliteration	Hebrew	Abbrev.
Sunday	Yom Ri-shon	יום א or יום ראשון	
Monday	Yom Shei-ni	יום ב or יום שני	
Tuesday	Yom She-li-shi	יום ג or יום שלישי	
Wednesday	Yom Re-vi-i	יום ד or יום רביעי	
Thursday	Yom Cha-mi-shi	יום ה or יום חמישי	
Friday	Yom Shi-shi	יום ו or יום שישי	
	E-rev Shab-bat	ערב שבת	עׄש
Friday after sunset	Leil Shab-bat	ליל שבת	
Saturday	Shab-bat	שבת	שׄ
	or Shab-bat Ko-desh	or שבת קודש	שׄק or
Saturday after sunset	Mo-tsi Shab-bat	מוצאי שבת	מוצׄ שׄ
	or Mo-tsi Shab-bat Ko-desh	or מוצאי שבת קודש	משׄק or

D. Years

While this section is really about Jewish calendar years, it is interesting to note that most monuments in the Diaspora include the Christian calendar date. However, it was only in 1992 that the Israel Supreme Court ruled that Jewish monument inscriptions in Israel may be in any language and may use dates of any calendar.

96

The syntax of the year is as follows:

| | i. | ii. |

<"In the year" or "in the year of" or nothing><numerical representation of year>

iii.

<by the Jewish calendar or nothing>

i. In the year

All the following occur, but most monuments do not explicitly state this.

In the year	Ba-sha-na	בשנה
In the year	De-sha-na	דשנה
In the year	La-sha-na	לשנה
In the year of	Bi-she-nat	בשנת
In the year of	Di-she-nat	דשנת
In the year of	Li-she-nat	לשנת
year of	yahr (Yiddish)	יאהר

ii. Numerical Representation of the year.

Chapter 3 provided a method of computing the Hebrew calendar year without dealing with the Hebrew alphabet. This section offers another method to compute the Hebrew calendar date, by computing the numerical value of the Hebrew letters that constitute the date. Each letter of the Hebrew alphabet has a numerical value. In most places on monuments where numbers are used, the Hebrew letters are used to represent numbers. However, there are monuments where the numbers are fully spelled out as words. Lists of fully spelled out numbers are not included in this book.

The following table is a list of the numerical values associated with Hebrew letters that are used to specify the year by the Hebrew calendar.

97

100	ק	10	י	1	א
200	ר	20	כ	2	ב
300	ש	30	ל	3	ג
400	ת	40	מ	4	ד
500*	ך	50	נ	5	ה
600*	ם	60	ס	6	ו
700*	ן	70	ע	7	ז
800*	ף	80	פ	8	ח
900*	ץ	90	צ	9	ט

There are 22 distinct letters in Hebrew. In addition, 5 letters have forms that are used only when they occur at the end of a word. These letters, labeled above with "*", are theoretically the larger numbers. In reality, they are not generally used on monuments. As a matter of fact, one common error one might see is the use of a final letter when it occurs at the end of a number. Example: 5720 represented as תש"ך rather than תש"כ.

The American Jewish experience places the oldest tombstones between 5300 and the current dates, now approaching 5800. The Hebrew years of death on monuments generally omit the "5000", although occasionally one may see the year of death led by the letter "ה". [See, "iii. By the Jewish Calendar" below.]

Accordingly, 800 will be represented by "תת"(i.e. 400 +400). 700 is represented by "תש" (i.e. 400+300), 600 by "תר" (i.e. 400+200) and 500 by "תק"(i.e. 400+100).

The remainder of the numbers are usually written in descending order, for example, 5743 would be represented as תשמ"ג, 743. There is considerable variation in whether an apostrophe or quotation marks are used to let the reader know that what they are seeing is not a word. Sometimes it will appear with neither as תשמג.

A notable exception is a year when the letter combination reads as a Hebrew word with a negative connotation. An example of this was 5744, תשמ"ד. "Tash-mad" means "destruction". Many (not all) monuments with תשמ"ד, "Tash-mad" as the year of death reversed the last two letters so that the inscription appears as תשד"מ (tash-dam).

Sometimes an effort is made to tell a story with the dates. On the monument of a man who lived to be 108 are the year of birth and the year of death. (Congregation Ohel Jacob of East Boston, Woburn, MA)

Common Year	Hebrew Year	Normal Year Syntax	As it appears on the monument
1814	5574	תְּקְעֵד	עי'קיד'ית'
1922	5682	תְּרְפֵּב	בי'פיר'ית'

The problem is, neither of the dates is either a well known acronym nor are they grammatically correct Hebrew words. Perhaps the context is that at birth we are bound and constricted (based on לעקד) and at death he was fully blossomed (based on פרות). In cases like this we find ourselves in the same position as those trying to decode vanity license plates on passing cars.

Also note that years such as 5715 and 5716 are often represented as 400+300+9+6 and 400+300+9+7. If the normal 10+5 were used for 15, or 10+6 for 16, the Hebrew letters would spell God's name. The tradition is therefore to use 9+6 for 15 and 9+7 for 16. Logically, there is no reason for doing this in designating the year. Once the letters of God's name are included in a greater string of letters, they could no longer be inadvertently mistaken for "taking God's name in vain." However, logic aside, tradition takes over. תשי"ה and תשי"ו are rare exceptions for 5715 and 5716. תשט"ו and תשט"ז are the norm for 5715 and 5716.

Dates can be abbreviated in many ways. All of the following are valid ways to represent 5759. The list is not exhaustive:

תשנט	היתשנט	ה תשנט

| תּשֹׁנֹט | הֹיתֹשֹׁנֹט | תשנ̃ט | היתשנ̃ט |

תישנ'ט	תשנ'ט	היתשני'ט

תשנ"ט	היתשנ"ט

---

iii. By the Jewish calendar

While some monuments explicitly note that the date given is "by the Jewish Calendar," most monuments assume that the reader already knows that. The following are the options for "by the Jewish Calendar":

By the Jewish Calendar   Lif-rat ga-dol   לפני" לפרט גדול

The full year is shown (i.e. 5743 will be shown as היתשמ'ג). [Less common than "לפק"]

By the Jewish Calendar   Lif-rat ka-tan   לפק" לפרט קטן

In the year "5XXX", only XXX will be shown (i.e. 5743 will be shown as תשמ'ג). This option is often abbreviated into the letters la-med, pei and kuf "לפק, which are often combined into the single icon below:

100

ק
‍
On most monuments, the use of "לפק" or its icon is straight-forward. The year is designated by the numbers that are written in descending order. For example, 5743 would be represented as תשמ"ג לפק", 743. But occasionally, you will see something like the following several examples:

Example #1:

וישכב דוד עם אבותיו לפק"

And David died (literally: slept with his fathers), 5476 by the Jewish Calendar.

Notice that three letters corresponding to the Jewish calendar date are mixed in with the epitaph and noted by the use of larger letters. The "5000" is omitted because it is "לפק". Tav(ת) equals 400; ayin(ע) equals 70; and vav(ו) equals 6.

Example #2:
The following Biblical quotation appeared on a monument of a man named Aaron who died in 5692(1932). If one adds up the numerical value of all of the letters that have a dot over them, 692 is the total.

ויראו כל העדה כי גוע אהרן
לפק"

And all the congregation saw that Aaron had died (Num. 20:29)
5692 by the Jewish Calendar

101

E. Date

The complete syntax of a date is as follows:

    i.   ii.   iii.   iv.
<On day><number><in the month of><name of month>

                  or

    v.
<holiday name>

                  or

both lines above.

When both the regular date (shown as i, ii, iii, iv) and the holiday (shown as v.) are both included sometimes the holiday is first and sometime it is second.

i. On Day
This is often omitted completely. When it appears it is as follows:

On day	be-yom	ביום
Day	Yom	יום
Day	Tag (Yiddish)	טאג or טעג

ii. Number
The day is usually given as a number shown in the table below. In most cases, the date is followed by the month. Dates often use an apostrophe, a quotation mark or nothing as shown below. In addition, a dot over each letter or a tilde (~) over the date are other ways of representing the date.

Below is shown the three most common representations of some numbers. A complete table was included in Chapter 3, "Monuments 101":

Table: Common representation of days of the month

1	א	אׂ	אׂ״	(1)
...				
10	י	יׂ	יׂ״	(10)
11	יא	יׂא	יׂ״א	(10+1)
...				
14	יד	יׂד	יׂ״ד	(10+4)
15	טו	טׂו	טׂ״ו	(9+6)
16	טז	טׂז	טׂ״ז	(9+7)
17	יז	יׂז	יׂ״ז	(10+7)
...				
20	כ	כׂ	כׂ״	(20)
21	כא	כׂא	כׂ״א	(20+1)
...				
30	ל	לׂ	לׂ״	(30)

If the normal 10+5 were used for 15, or 10+6 for 16, the Hebrew letters would spell one of God's names. The tradition is therefore to use 9+6 for 15 and 9+7 for 16. Occasionally, the non-traditional format sneaks through. (Much less often, the number of the day will actually be included rather than the numerical equivalents shown above. E.g. ... ששת ימים לחודש..., ...sixth day of the month of...)

Note: Occasionally, the order of i. and ii. will reverse.
Examples:

19th day of ...	yod-tet yom	י״ט יום
19th day of ...	yod-tet ya-mim	י״ט ימים

iii. in the month of
This is often omitted completely. When it appears it is as follows:

In the month of	ba-cho-desh	בחדש or בחודש
In the moon(month) of	ba-ya-rei-ach	בירח
In the month of	de-cho-desh	דחדש or דחודש
In the moon(month) of	de-ya-rei-ach	דירח
In the month of	la-cho-desh	לחדש or לחודש
In the moon(month) of	la-ya-rei-ach	לירח

iv. Name of Month
The list of months that follows presents much more details that the one provided in Chapter 5:

A List of Months

Note: Corresponding earliest dates and latest dates between Hebrew Calendar months and common calendar reflect the years between 1785 and 2000 CE.

Tishri   תשרי
(Begins as early as September 5 or as late as October 5.)
Cheshvan   חשון or חשוון
Also known as **Marcheshvan**   מרחשון or מרחשוון
(Begins as early as October 5 or as late as November 4.)
Kislev   כסלו
(Begins as early as November 3 or as late as December 3.)
Tevet   טבת
(Begins as early as December 2 or as late as January 2.)
Shevat   שבט
(Begins as early as December 31 or as late as January 31.)
Adar (or Adar Alef   אדר ראשון or אדר א' or אדר
Adar 1 or Adar I or Adar Rishon)
(Begins as early as January 30 or as late as March 2.)

Adar Bet (or Adar Shei-ni   אדר ב' or אדר שני or ואדר

    Adar 2 or Adar II or Ve-Adar)

    (Begins as early as March 1 or as late as March 13.)

Nisan or **Aviv**   אביב or ניסן or נסן

    (Begins as early as March 12 or as late as April 11.)

Iyar   אייר or איר

    (Begins as early as April 11 or as late as May 11.)

Sivan   סיון or סיוון

    (Begins as early as May 10 or as late as June 9.)

Tammuz   תמוז

    (Begins as early as June 9 or as late as July 9.)

Av   מנחם אב or אב

    Also known as Menachem Av[13]   מנ' אב or מנ'א or

                                           מ'א or מ'אב or

    (Begins as early as July 8 or as late as August 7.)

Elul   אלול

    (Begins as early as August 7 or as late as September 6.)

---

[13] On the ninth of the month of Av, the fast of Av, *Ti-shah Be-Av*, occurs. *Ti-shah Be-Av* commemorates the destruction of the Temples in Jerusalem. *Me-na-chem*, meaning comfort, is sometimes added to the name of month of Av. According to tradition, on dates prior to *Ti-shah Be-Av*, the month is referred to as Av. After *Ti-shah Be-Av*, the month is referred to as *Me-na-chem Av*. However, on monuments, *Me-na-chem Av* and Av are both found, regardless of whether the date is before or after *Ti-shah Be-Av*.

Some Examples of Complete date lines without Holidays

Example 1

Died <day of week>	Died on Saturday,	נפ" ביום ש"ק
<date> <month>	the 27th of She-vat	כ"ז שבט
<year>	5681	תרפ"א

Example 2.
Note the potential ambiguity:

Died <day of week>	Died on Friday,	נפ" ביום ו'
<date> <month>	the 26th of She-vat	כ"ו בשבט
<year>	5681	תרפ"א

versus

| Died <date> | Died on the 6th day | נפ" ביום ו' |
| <month> <year> | of She-vat 5681 | בשבט תרפ"א |

If two numbers are together, the syntax is the "day of the week," followed by "day of the month". The same is true if ביום appears twice. If only one number follows ביום, the number is a "day of the month".

Example 3.
In this example, everything is clearly spelled out. Note that any combination of the words underlined may be omitted.

Died <day of the week>, day <"x">, of the month <"y">, of year <year> by the Jewish calendar.

Died on <u>Monday</u>,	נפ" ביום שני
<u>day</u> 28	ביום כ"ח
<u>of the month of</u> Nisan	דחדש (or דירח) ניסן
<u>of the year</u> 5734	דשנת תשל"ד
<u>by the Jewish calendar.</u>	לפק"

v. Dates by Holiday Name

If the death occurred on a holiday, the holiday is sometimes given either in lieu of or in addition to the Hebrew calendar date. In the listing, the letter "ד" is shown as optional. However, a "ב", "לי" or "של" will often appear in the spot where the "ד" is shown.

The vast majority of time, the Hebrew letters are used in lieu of numbers. But occasionally you will find:

On the second day of ...	Be-yom shei-ni shel...	ביום שני של ...

I have examined thousands of head stones. With 385 possible Hebrew dates to choose from and many ways of representing them, it is nearly impossible to check out the possibilities exhaustively. I do not claim to have seen every entry in the table below. However, I did encounter one that said "Shushan Purim Katan", which was so obscure that I erred on the side of caution to include it and other obscure possibilities.

The calendar for the Jews of the Diaspora is slightly different than the calendar for Jews living in Israel for Sukkot, Passover and Shavuot. The information in the table that follows is for the Orthodox/Conservative Jewish holidays in the Diaspora. Appendix A contains both the Israeli variations and the Reform variations.

Table of Holiday Designations

New Moon	Rosh Cho-desh	ראש חדש	ר"ח
Eve of	E-rev	ערב	ע'
Eve of New Moon	E-rev Rosh Cho-desh (29th of the month except Elul)	ערב ראש חדש	ער"ח
Little Day of Atonement	Yom Kippur Katan (29th of the month except Nisan, Kislev, Elul and Tishri)	יום כפור קטן	יכ"ק
New Moon	Rosh Chodesh (when one day)	[ד]ראש חדש	[ד][ר"ח]

When New Moon is 2 days:

30ᵗʰ of the previous month is 1ˢᵗ Day	א [ד]ראש חדש א [ד]ר"ח
First of the new month is 2ⁿᵈ Day	ב [ד]ראש חדש ב [ד]ר"ח

(Note: For Rosh Chodesh to be unambiguous, the name of the month must also be stated.)

Passover	Pe-sach (15 Nisan)	פסח	פ'
Day before Passover	14 Nisan	ערב [ד]פסח	ע[ד]פ'
	15 Nisan (after sunset, before midnight)	ליל [ד]פסח	
1st day	15 Nisan	א [ד]פסח	א [ד]פ'
2nd day	16 Nisan	ב [ד]פסח	ב [ד]פ'
**3rd day[14]	17 Nisan	א [ד]חול המועד פסח	א [ד]חהפ'
**4th day	18 Nisan	ב [ד]חול המועד פסח	ב [ד]חהפ'
**5th day	19 Nisan	ג [ד]חול המועד פסח	ג [ד]חהפ'
**6th day	20 Nisan	ד [ד]חול המועד פסח	ד [ד]חהפ'

---

[14] **The longer holidays, specifically Passover and Sukkot, contain four "semi-holidays" referred to as "the intermediate days" in English, or *chol ha-mo-eid* in Hebrew. [While Sukkot theoretically has 5 intermediate days, the fifth is usually referred to as *Ho-sha-na Ra-bah*.] All of the following are variations of the abbreviation for *Chol ha-mo-eid*. Apostrophes are shown, but quotes, dots, tildes, etc. indicating an abbreviation can occur in numerous places in the acronym or not at all:

חוהמו' דחוהמו' חוהמ' דחוהמ' חה' דחה'

108

7th day	21 Nisan	ז [ד]פסח	ז [ד]פ׳
8th day	22 Nisan	ח [ד]פסח	ח [ד]פ׳
Last day of Passover	22 Nisan	יום אחרון [ד]פסח	
	23 Nisan (after sunset, before midnight)	מוצאי פסח	
First day after Passover Is-ru chag Pesach	23 Nisan	אסרו חג [ד]פסח	אח[ן]ד[פ

| Omer | Omer | עומר |

The omer is the counting of the 49 days of the days between Passover and Shavuot. The omer was an offering of barley to the ancient Temple at Passover and linked Passover to Shavuot. In theory, the number associated with the count of the omer could be any number between 1 and 49. But one thru seven would more likely be referred to as Passover; the 8th would be Is-ru Chag Passover, the 15th and 16th are Rosh Chodesh Iyar, the 45th is Rosh Chodesh Sivan and, the 49 is Erev Shavuot.

9th day of the Omer	24 Nisan	ט׳ [ב]עומר
...	....	
33rd day of the Omer	Lag BaOmer (18 Iyar)	ל׳ג בעומר
...	....	
36th day of the Omer	La-med vav baOmer (21 Iyar)	ל׳ו [ב]עומר
...	....	
48th day of the Omer	4 Sivan	מח [ב]עומר

Feast of Weeks	Shavuot	שבועות	ש׳
Day before Shavuot	5 Sivan	ערב]ד[שבועות	ע]ד[ש׳
	6 Sivan (after sunset, before midnight)	ליל]ד[שבועות	
1st day	6 Sivan	א]ד[שבועות	
2nd day	7 Sivan	ב]ד[שבועות	
	8 Sivan (after sunset, before midnight)	מוצאי שבועות	
First day after Shavuot	8 Sivan Is-ru Chag Shavuot	אסרו חג]ד[שבועות	אח׳]ד[ש

New Year	Rosh Hashannah	ראש השנה	ר׳ה
Eve of Rosh Hashannah	29 Elul Erev Rosh Hashannah	ערב]ד[ראש השנה	ע]ד[ר׳ה
	1 Tishri (after sunset, before midnight)	ליל]ד[ראש השנה	
1st day	1 Tishri	א]ד[ר׳ה א]ד[ראש השנה	
2nd day	2 Tishri	ב]ד[ר׳ה ב]ד[ראש השנה	
	3 Tishri (after sunset, before midnight)	מ׳]ד[ר׳ה מוצאי]ד[ראש השנה	
Fast of Gedaliah	3 Tishri	צום גדליה	צ׳ג׳

Day of Atonement	Yom Kippur	יום כפור	י׳כ
Eve of Yom Kippur	Erev Yom Kippur 9 Tishri	ערב]ד[יום כפור	ע]ד[י׳כ
	10 Tishri (after sunset, before midnight)	ליל יום כפור)הכפורים(	
Day of Atonement	Yom Kippur 10 Tishri	יום כפור)יום הכפורים(	י׳כ
	11 Tishri (after sunset, before midnight)	מוצאי יום כפור	מוצ׳יו׳כפ׳

Feast of Tabernacles	15 Tishri Sukkot	סוכות or סכות	ס'
Eve of Sukkot	14 Tishri 15 Tishri (after sunset, before midnight)	ערב [ד]סוכות ליל [ד]סוכות	ע[ד]ס'
1st day	15 Tishri	א [ד]סוכות	א [ד]ס'
2nd day	16 Tishri	ב [ד]סוכות	ב [ד]ס'
**3rd day[15]	17 Tishri	א [ד]חול המועד סוכות	א [ד]חהס'
**4th day	18 Tishri	ב [ד]חול המועד סוכות	ב [ד]חהס'
**5th day	19 Tishri	ג [ד]חול המועד סוכות	ג [ד]חהס'
**6th day	20 Tishri	ד [ד]חול המועד סוכות	ד [ד]חהס'
Seventh day of Sukkot	Ho-sha-na Rab-bah 21 Tishri	הושענא רבא	
Eighth day of Sukkot	She-mi-ni A-tse-ret 22 Tishri	שמיני עצרת	ש"ע
Ninth day of Sukkot	Sim-chat Torah 23 Tishri	שמחת [ה]תורה	ש"ת
	24 Tishri (after sunset, before midnight)	מוצאי [ד]סוכות	מ"ס
First day after Sukkot	24 Tishri Is-ru Chag Sukkot	אסרו חג [ד]סוכות	אח"ס
Chanukah	Chanukah	חנכה or חנוכה	
Eve of Chanuka	24 Kislev	ערב [ד]חנכה	
1st day	25 Kislev	א [ד]חנכה	
2nd day	26 Kislev	ב [ד]חנכה	
3rd day	27 Kislev	ג [ד]חנכה	
4th day	28 Kislev	ד [ד]חנכה	
5th day	29 Kislev	ה [ד]חנכה	
6th day	30 Kislev (1 Tevet)	ו [ד]חנכה	
7th day	1 Tevet (2 Tevet)	ז [ד]חנכה	
8th day	2 Tevet (3 Tevet)	ח [ד]חנכה	

---

[15] See footnote above on Passover

111

Note: Depending on the year, Kislev may be either 29 or 30 days long. The parentheticals refer to years when there is no 30th of Kislev.

Feast of Lots	Purim	פורים
Little Feast of Lots	Purim Ka-tan 14 Adar Alef (in a leap year)	פורים קטן
Little Feast of Lots in Shushan	Shushan Purim Ka-tan 15 Adar Alef (in a leap year)	שושן פורים קטן
Fast of Esther	Ta-a-nit Esther 13 Adar	תענית אסתר
Feast of Lots	Purim 14 Adar (14 Adar Bet if a leap year)	פורים
Feast of Lots in Shushan	Shu-shan Purim 15 Adar (15 Adar Bet if a leap year)	שושן פורים

Examples of Dates which include holidays:

Example 1. Holiday given in lieu of the date.

Died <day of week>	Died on Sunday	נפ" ביום א"
day <"x"> of <holiday>	second intermediate	ב" דחה"ס
<year>	day of Sukkot, 5734	תשל"ד

Example 2. Holiday given in addition to the date.

Died <day of week>	Died on Sunday	נפ" ביום א"
day <"x"> of <holiday>	second interme- diate day of Sukkot	ב" דחה"ס
<date><month>	18th of Tishri,	י"ח תשרי
<year>	5734	תשל"ד

Example 3. Everything about the day and date is spelled out in the example below. The underlined words could be omitted without compromising the uniqueness of the date.

> Died <day of the week>, holiday, day <"x">, of the month <"y">, of year <year> according to the Jewish Calendar.

Example:

<u>Died on Monday,</u>	נפ" ביום ב'
Third day, chol ha-mo-eid Sukkot	ג" דחה"ס
<u>day 19</u>	ביום י"ט
<u>of the month of Tishri</u>	דחדש תשרי
<u>of the year 5734</u>	דשנת תשל"ד
<u>by the Jewish calendar.</u>	לפק"

F. Age of the Deceased

Most monuments include enough information to determine the age of the deceased. Sometimes, the common calendar dates of both birth and death are included. Less frequently, both the date of birth and death are given in the Jewish Calendar as described earlier in this chapter.

This section is a format when a specific age is specified. When it is given, it appears in the following format:

```
    i.          ii.         iii.        iv.         v.
<Died><at age of><number><years><of his/her life>
```

i. Died (masc.) nif-tar נפטר נפ"
   Died (fem.) nif-te-ra נפטרה נפ"

ii. At the age of

	ben	בן	ב'
	bat	בת	ב'
	be-gil	בגיל	
	ge-tsilt	(Yiddish) געצילט	

113

iii. Year: See Table under "Years", (Chapter 7. D. ii.)

iv. Years   sha-na or sha-nim   שנה or שנים

v. Optional - often omitted

    Of his life   ye-mei cha-yav   ימי חייו   י"ח

    Of her life   ye-mei cha-ya   ימי חייה   י"ח

Example:

 A man who died at age 84:

         iv.   iii. ii. i.   v.   iv. iii. ii. i.

      נפ' בן פ'ד שנה ימי חייו   or   נפ' בן פ'ד שנה

Alternative option:

   The years of his life were...   she-nei ye-mei cha-yav...   ...שני ימי חייו

   The years of his life were...   she-nei cha-yav...   ...שני חייו

   All the years of his life were...   kol she-nei   ...כל שני ימי חייו

                                 ye-mei cha-yav...

Note: Substitute חייה for חייו for "her life".

The above options are most often followed by a number of years, but the example below carries it to months and days.

Example:

From the Old Jewish Cemetery, Newport, RI:

The days of her life were 65   שני חייה ס"ה

 years, 6 months, 18 days   שנים ו' חדשים י"ח ימים

Other oddball dates:

This section is potentially unlimited and is presented more as a few examples. It clearly demonstrates that while the format of a date can be generally categorized to include 99+% of the possibilities, there are many interesting twists lurking out there in the Jewish cemeteries of the world.

By the Torah Portion:

A section of the Torah is read each week at the synagogue. A week is often designated by the name of the Torah portion read that week. The new week's Torah portion is previewed at the Saturday afternoon service. Less than a tenth of a percent of monuments include this information. However, among those that do, two choices occur. Most of the time the portion designated is the actual portion of the week in which the deceased died. But sometimes, the Torah portion named is the last one completed before death. To list all the *pa-ra-shi-yot* (sections of the Torah) would be beyond the scope of this volume. The key to this is the notation "פ" in the date line.

Example:

Parshat Be-har/Be-chu-ko-tai פרשת בהר-בבחקותי   פ' בה"ב

Unusual Holiday Combination

The date that follows is unusual, because it happens to occur only in years when the first day of Passover happens to be Shabbat. The example below is merely saying "He died on the 8th day of Passover."

Died on the last Sabbath   נפטר בשק אחרון

of Passover, year of 5681   של פסח שנת תרפא

Specifying Daylight or night

References to nighttime following a holiday or Sabbath is relatively common and was included in the table of holiday and holiday abbreviations. The following phrase specified that death occurred during daylight hours:

... during the light..   ... or le-yom ...   ... אור ליום ...

of the day of...

Inconsistent Use of Abbreviation Marks

The date that follows is a good example of the inconsistencies in cemetery inscriptions. First, there was no mark to identify the acronym, *Erev Shabbat Kodesh* (עשק) or the year (תרעט) but there was to identify the new moon (*Rosh Chodesh* ר"ח).

Died on Friday (Eve of Sabbath)	נפטר יום עשק
1 Rosh Chodesh 1st Adar5679	א ר"ח אדר א תרעט

No abbreviation Marks

The following date is presented exactly as it appeared. Below it, is a version with appropriately placed abbreviation marks that make it a little easier to read:

Died 29th of Tishri 5741	נפ כט תשרי תשמא
	נפ' כט' תשרי תשמ'א

By the Common Calendar

Often the Hebrew calendar date will be transliterated into Roman characters. The case where the common calendar date (i.e. the Gregorian date) is transliterated into Hebrew letters is unusual, but it occurs.

Date of Death/Date of Burial

Most monuments give just the date of death. Some monuments include the date of birth. By Jewish custom, the date of burial is usually the same as the day of death or within a day. There are cases where the difference is unusually long. One example is when the deceased is deemed "missing in action." Alternatively, war casualties were sometimes buried at the battlefield and moved to private cemeteries after the war was over. In both of these cases, there may be several years between date of death and date of burial and this is sometimes noted.

Se-li-chot

Other than Shabbat, Se-li-chot is the only Jewish calendar event that is specified as a day of the week as opposed to a specific date. The days of Se-li-chot always begins on Sunday.

Rosh Hashannah (RH) Starts:	Se-li-chot begins on Sunday
Sunday PM/Monday AM	Elul 22 (8 days before RH)
Monday PM/Tuesday AM	Elul 21 (9 days before RH)
Wednesday PM/Thursday AM	Elul 26 (4 days before RH)
Friday PM/Saturday AM	Elul 24 (6 days before RH)

Se-li-chot is a set of prayers said in preparation for the High Holydays. The traditional time for the service is mid-night, but Reform and Conservative synagogues often have the services earlier.

The following inscription (Anshe Poland, Woburn, MA) is unusual in that it names both the date of death and the date of burial and that it specifically notes the date of burial as "the Sunday of Se-li-chot".

Died on the 23rd of
   the month of Elul
and was buried on the
   Sunday of Se-li-chot
in the year of 5689.

מתה ביום כ"ג לחודש אלול

ונקברה ביום א דסליחות

שנת תרפט
Sep. 28, 1929

8. Epitaphs – Standard

Decoration:	פ ✡ נ
Introductory Line:	אבינו היקר
Name Line:	יצחק בן יוסף
Dateline:	נפ" כ"ח ניסן תשל"ז
	Isaac Stone
	Died April 16, 1977
Epitaph:	תנצב"ה

The potential for epitaphs is unlimited. Often, epitaphs are verses from the Bible or other Jewish texts. Sometimes, they are interchangeable in monument format with "The Introductory Line" (Chapter 5). The vast majority of epitaphs are generic statements or biblical quotations that emphasize character qualities of the person.

This chapter deals only with the most standard epitaphs. For the purpose of this book, an epitaph is defined as any writing on the monument not specific to the name of the deceased and date(s) associated with the life of the deceased.

The longer epitaphs include acrostics and lengthy passages of all sorts. These are dealt with separately in chapters 9 and 10.

The Simplest Epitaphs

Chapter 3 suggested the following as the three most common epitaphs. One of these will be found on more than 75% of all monuments with epitaphs:

Let his (her) soul	Te-hi naf-sho (naf-sha)	תנצב"ה
be bound up	tsa-ru-ra	
in the bonds of.	be-tse-rur ha-cha-yim.	
the living	(Adapted from1 Sam. 25:29)	

| May his (her) memory be a blessing (Based on Prov. 10:7) | Zich-ro-no (Zich-ro-na) le-ve-ra-cha | ז"ל |
| May the memory of the righteous be a blessing (Prov. 10:7) | Zei-cher tsa-dik le-ve-ra-cha | זצ"ל |

Beyond these three, תנצב"ה, ז"ל and זצ"ל, we also have:

He will rest in peace	Ya-nu-ach	ינוח	יבע"מ
	Be-sha-lom	בשלום	
	Al mish-ka-vo	על משכבו	

(from *"Eil ma-lei ra-cha-mim"* prayer)

| Peace | Shalom | שלום |
| The late ...(name follows) | Ha-ma-nu-ach | המנוח |

The following is very simple, but not common:

| So be it | Amen | אמן |

Shalom appears more frequently on recent monuments. Shalom means "hello", "good bye" and "peace." Some have suggested that it is intended to wish "peace" to the individual buried there. Others have suggested that its purpose is for the living to say goodbye to the deceased. Still others have suggested that as more Americans know less Hebrew, *shalom* is one Hebrew word to which even the most assimilated Jew can relate. The last statement also applies to the epitaph "amen."

Sephardic cemeteries will sometimes use the Spanish or Ladino acronym, SBAGDG which stands for "sua bendita alma goze de gloria", meaning "May his blessed soul enjoy glory" or SAGDG, which stands for "sua alma goze de gloria", meaning "May his soul enjoy glory".

Abbreviations:

Abbreviations or honorifics, pertaining to the deceased, show up in various places on monuments, with no particular syntax.

My master, my father	A-do-ni a-vi	אדוני אבי	א"א
God willing	Be-ez-rat ha-shem	בעזרת השם	ב"ה
With the help of God	be-si-yu-a ha-shem	בסיוע השם	בס"ה
God (tetragrammaton)[16]	A-do-nai or ha-shem	יהוה "ה or "ד
Let his(her) rest	Nu-cho	נוחו	נ"ע
be Paradise	(nu-cha) ei-den	(נוחה) עדן	
Rest in Peace	A-lav (A-le-ha)	עליו	ע"ה
	ha-sha-lom.	(עליה) השלום	

Biblical - Tanach (תנ"ך):

Many epitaphs are either from the Bible or derived from the Bible. The potential list that individuals might choose to include is unlimited; however, the most common source for monument quotes is Psalms and Proverbs. While that is generally true, the following are the most common biblical citations:

Most common for men:
 Some combination or expansion of Lamentations 5:16-17

 The crown of our head. A-te-ret ro-shei-nu   עטרת ראשנו
 (Lam. 5:16)

---

[16] There are some Jews who believe that writing the word "God" is taking God's name in vain. These people will write 'G-d' in lieu of God. The same occurs in Hebrew, where אלהים will be written as אלקים and the tetragrammaton (four letter name of God), יהוה, will be written as "ה" or "ד." "ה" stands for השם (ha-shem) which mean "the name." "ד" has the numerical value of '4' and is a reference to the fact that God's proper name has four letters.

For this we are sad	Al zeh	עַל זֶה
(sick at heart),	da-veh li-bei-nu	דָּוֶה לִבֵּנוּ
For this	al ei-leh	עַל אֵלֶּה
our eyes are dimmed.	cho-she-chu ei-nei-nu	חָשְׁכוּ עֵינֵינוּ
(Lam. 5:17)		

Most common for women:
Some or all of the section known as "the woman of valor",
Ei-shet cha-yil (אשת חייל), Prov. 31:10-31.

Most common for couples:

Beloved and cherished,	Ha-ne-e-ha-vim	הַנֶּאֱהָבִים
	ve-ha-ne-e-ma-nim	וְהַנְּעִימִם
in life, and in death,	ba-cha-yei-hem	בְּחַיֵּיהֶם
	u-ve-mo-tam	וּבְמוֹתָם
they were not parted.	lo nif-re-du.	לֹא נִפְרָדוּ
(2 Sam. 1:23)		

NOTE: It is interesting that this text's context was not referring to a man and a woman, but to David and Jonathan.

Biblical: Specific to the name of the deceased

Many Biblical quotes link the deceased to the biblical character whose name they share. The following is example is specific to Noah.

| Noah walked | Et ha-e-lo-him | אֶת הָאֱלֹהִים |
| with God.(Gen. 6:9) | hit-ha-leich No-ach. | הִתְהַלֶּךְ נֹחַ |

Quotations of this sort can be found referring to Abraham (Gen. 22:11), Sarah (Gen. 23:2), Isaac (Gen. 25:20, Gen. 25:29), Rachel (Gen. 35:20), Jacob (Gen. 46:2), Joseph (Gen. 42:36), Moses (Ex. 2:4), Miriam (Nu. 20:1), Aaron (Nu. 20:29), Deborah (Ju. 5:12), Samuel (1 Sam. 3:4), David (1 Ki. 2:10, 1 Chron. 17:24) and Esther (Esth. 2:15, Esth. 8:4). To those with minimal Hebrew skills, the clue here is to look for the person's Hebrew name in the epitaph.

Sometimes, the name is the epitaph as in (Samuel 1 25:25):

He epitomized his name   Ki-she-mo kein hu   כשמו כן הוא

She epitomized her name   Ki-she-ma kein hi   כשמה כן היא

Children's Monuments:

Children's monuments are usually small, plain and rarely have more than a name and a date. When they do have more, it is often to reflect on the youthfulness of the child. Other phrases follow:

An only child	ben ya-chid	בן יחיד
A dear young man (Gen. 49:22)	Ben po-rat	בן פרת
A pet child (Jer. 31:19)	Ye-led sha-a-shu-im	ילד שעשועים
A young branch	A-naf ra-a-nan	ענף רענן
A flower cut off	Pe-rach ka-tuf	פרח קטוף

Hamadrikh

Hamadrikh[17], the best known of the Rabbi's manuals has a section on inscriptions, but there is no translation of the inscriptions. Because of the ubiquity of that book, those are now among the most common inscriptions found on post 1940 monuments. The translations to the 18 inscriptions in Hamadrikh are presented in Appendix B.

Superlatives often associated with Rabbis:

Congregations love their rabbis. Their death brings out superlatives. This, by the way, is not generally reflective of the ego of the deceased but of the relationship of the survivors or the community to deceased.

---

[17] Goldin, *Hamadrikh* (Hebrew Publishing Co., New York, NY, 1939)

Master of the (religious) court	Av beit din	אב"ד אב בית דין
My master, my teacher & my rabbi	A-do-ni Mo-ri ve-ra-bi	אדמו"ר אדוני מורי ורבי
Our master, our, teacher our rabbi	A-do-nei-nu Mo-rei-nu ve-ra-bei-nu	אדמו"ר אדוננו מורנו ורבנו
The great scholar	He-cha-cham ha-ga-dol	ה"ה החכם הגדול
The sainted Rabbi	Ha-rav ha-tsa-dik	הרה"צ הרב הצדיק
Our honored master, scholar, rabbi	Ke-vod Mo-rei-nu he-cha-cham ra-bi	כמהור"ר כבוד מורנו החכם רבי

In much of the Jewish world, the gradations in titles among members of the Jewish clergy do appear on monuments. However, in North America, the rabbinic title is relatively egalitarian and differences in titles don't usually appear on monuments. There are two major exceptions that do appear frequently on monuments. First, a non-ordained lay leader will be referred to a Reverend (Rev.) and Sephardim refer to their rabbis as "*He-cha-cham* (החכם)."

Talmudic:

The Talmud is a major source of Jewish Law and lore. References to it in Jewish life abound. It is no surprise that monuments contain materials from there. The following, both in Aramaic, are the most common examples:

| What is hateful to you do not do to your neighbor. (Shabbat 31a) | de-a-leich se-ni le-cha-vei-reich lo ta-a-vid | דעלך סני לחברך לא תעביד |
| Woe for the loss and let us not forget. (Sanhedrin 111a) | Cha-val al de-av-din ve-lo mish-ta-che-chin. | חבל על דאבדין ולא משתכחין |

The context of the above quote is God speaking to Moses about Moses' ancestors, Abraham, Isaac and Jacob.

Prayers and Liturgy

Like Biblical phrases, prayer is a link between people and God. The use of familiar phrases from prayers is another meaningful way to remember the deceased. The most common is the *Shema*.

Key Words to Get the Sense of an Epitaph

The following are categories of short epitaphs, with one or two key words to identify the category of an epitaph:

1. Commandments: (Key Hebrew Word: Mitsvot - מצות)
One purpose of a Jewish life is to make the world a better place. The concept is known as "perfecting the world" or "*Tikun O-lam*" [תקון עולם]. Observing Mitsvot is a method by which Jews try to make the world better.

2. Commandments: Charity (Key Hebrew Word: Tse-da-kah - צדקה)
Charity and charitability are mitsvot, but since there are quite a few references specific to *tse-da-kah*, it is included as a separate category.

3. Commandments: Ritually Observant (Key Hebrew Word: *Sho-mer* - שומר)
Being ritually observant is a subset of commandments (Mitsvot), but these epitaphs associated with ritual observance often include the word *sho-mer*.

4. Family and community (Key Hebrew Word: *Mish-pa-chah* – משפחה)
Epitaphs frequently reflect the deceased's relationship to his/her family and community. Look for the word *mish-pa-chah*.

125

5. God: Relationship with (Key Hebrew Word: *Yi-ra* - ירא)

Epitaphs sometimes describe something about the deceased's relationship with God. The most common word to look for is *yi-ra*, meaning "fear," usually in the context of fearing God.

6. Length of Life (Key Hebrew Words: *Sha-na, sha-nim, she-not* – שנה, שנים, שנות)

The vast majority of monuments that include age information do so in the date line, usually specifying a specific number of years. Epitaphs of this category would suggest the person was very young, very old, etc.

While many monuments mention the length of life and take great pride in a long life, occasionally there are those too proud to mention it. Our society tends to think of women as being more vain about age then men. However, the following example is from a man's monument:

| Older than 30 years! | Yo-ter mi-she-lo-shim sha-na | יותר משלשים שנה |

7. Lineage *(Yi-chas)*: (Key Hebrew Word: Ben [בן] appears multiple times)

The Jewish concept of "*ze-chut a-vot*", the merit of the fathers, lets us know that we can accrue benefits based on whom our ancestors are. Reflecting that concept, inscriptions sometimes include not only the name of the father of the deceased, but also the grandfather's name.

8. Memory of the Deceased: Blessing (Key Hebrew Word: *Zei-cher* - זכר)

The guarantee of Jewish immortality is the way the deceased are remembered by those who survive them. The phrases in this category are reflective that the deceased is still impacting the living.

9. Memory of the Deceased: Honor (Key Hebrew Word: *Ka-vod* - כבוד)

Honor is a subset of the memories left behind by the deceased.

10. Memory of the Deceased: Righteousness (Key Hebrew Word: *Che-sed* - חסד)

Righteousness is another one of the virtues that the dead carries to the grave that helps make the memory of the deceased a blessing.

11. Resurrection of the Dead (Key Hebrew Words: *Te-chi-yat ha-mei-tim* - תחיית המתים)

Resurrection of the dead is a widely held Jewish belief. However, relatively few epitaphs choose this theme.

12. Spirit/Soul (Key Hebrew Words: *ru-ach, ne-fesh, ne-sha-ma* – רוח, נפש, נשמה)

The soul is eternal, but different monuments that mention the soul choose a number of different ways to describe it. The concept is that the earth is the physical home and that the heavens are the spiritual home of the soul.

13. Tears (Key Hebrew Words: *Ei-vel, di-mah, bo-che, ne-hi* - אבל, דמעה, בוכה, נהי)

Grief and mourning are often expressed with tears. Epitaphs emphasizing mourning often include the lament, *ei-vel*; tear, *di-mah*; cry, *bocheh;* wail, *ne-hi* in the inscription.

14. Wisdom (Key Hebrew Word: *Choch-mah* - חכמה)

Wisdom is one of the cornerstones of Judaism. Many of the epitaphs emphasizing wisdom feature the word, *choch-mah*.

15. World to come (Key Hebrew Words: *O-lam ha-ba, Ei-den* - עולם הבא, עדן)

The meaning of the term, "World to Come" is unclear and interpreted in many ways in the Jewish world. Judaism offers no dogmas of a "world to come" sometimes called *Ei-den* or *Gan Ei-den* (Paradise or the Garden of Eden).   There is a substantial body of literature and midrashic materials on the "world to come."   However, the only guarantee is that we will be remembered by the living for those things we did in our lifetimes.   This is reflected in the acronym "תַּנְצְבָ"ה that was discussed previously. Despite this concept, many epitaphs and phrases from epitaphs emphasize the "world to come" or "Eden."

16. Zionism (Key Hebrew Words: *Tsiyon*, Hadassah – צִיּוֹן, הֲדַסָּה)

The twentieth century has yielded a strong sense of Zionism. This category includes examples of people who are remembered in part for their attachment to Zionism.   The key words are *Tsiyon*, meaning Zion and Hadassah, the name of the largest women's Zionist movement.

Sometimes Israel (יִשְׂרָאֵל) will indicate a Zionist epitaph.   But Israel is also a very common first name and therefore appears often on the monuments of those who have no tie or minimal tie to Zionism.

9. Acrostics, Poetry and Other Longer Epitaphs

Previous chapters have focused on teaching the reader how to decode monuments. This section goes well beyond that scope. Understanding these inscriptions requires a fairly good command of Hebrew. As a result, no transliterations are included in this section. To capture a lifetime in a few sentences or even a paragraph is impossible but the following inscriptions show that many try to leave more than their name and date of death.

Acrostics

An acrostic is a series of lines or verses in which the first, last or other particular letters form a word or phrase. Epitaphs emphasize the deceased's relationship to survivors, a summary of the deceased's life's work, or a hope for the peace of the deceased. Six examples follow that give a cross-section of the major variants of acrostics.

Short, sweet and maybe even unintentional (Austrian Cemetery Association, Woburn, MA).

Most times when acrostics occur, they are obvious and intended. The word spelled out by the acrostic is clearly the person's name or the characters constituting the acrostic are set off in a way that makes it apparent that this is an acrostic. The following example may have been unintended.

Father אבא
If this acrostic was intentional, the only clue is the formatting. The inscription is presented twice below. The first time, it is presented as it actually appears on the monument. The second time, the inscription is reformatted as described in Chapter 3, "Monuments 101[18]."

---

[18] Note, the fact that the man was 46 years old is not included in Chapter 3 and would require a look at Chapter 7, Section f.

Here lies

פ׳ ✡ נ׳

Our beloved father Eliezer	אבינו היקר אליעזר
son of Mr. She-mu-eil	ברי שמואל נפטר ו׳
(Samuel). Died 6th	
Adar 5688 (1928) at age 46	אדר תרפח בן מו
years. Let his soul...	שנה תנצצב׳ה׳

Here lies

Our beloved father	אבינו היקר
Eliezer son of Mr. She-mu-eil (Samuel).	אליעזר בר׳ שמואל
Died 6th Adar 5688	נפטר ו׳ אדר תרפח בן מו שנה
(1928) at age 46 years.	
Let his soul...	תנצצב׳ה׳

Sequential Words

The author of this acrostic inscription has carefully chosen the first six words to spell out the name of the deceased. It is also different from the other acrostics in this chapter because the method for indicating the acrostic was superscripting.

<u>A woman named Judith (Ye-hu-dit יהודית)</u> (Anshe Lebovits, Woburn, MA)

Sons and daughters cry	יבכו הבנים והבנות
that the beloved of their	דנלקה יקר תפארתם
glory was stricken.	
Our beloved and modest mother	אמנו היקרה והצנועה
Yehudit daughter of	יהודית בר פנחס זעליג
Mr. Pinchas Zelig	
Died 5 Tishri 5674 (1914)	נפ׳ ה׳ תשרי תרעד
Let her soul...	תנצבה

130

Sentence Demarcation

The following acrosric inscription is an example where a distraught parent buried his child. It appeared on a monument for a 27-year-old named Naphtali (Framingham-Natick, Massachusetts.) The only English appearing on this stone was the name, "N. H. Brown". There is no spare space on the stone. The large letters, spelling Naphtali, are the sentence delimiters.

Monument   גלעד

Mighty wrestlings,   נ‎פתולי אלהים נפתלתי **פ**רי גני

I have wrestled (Gen. 30:8).
The fruit of my garden

and a beloved son have   ת‎אנתי על מות ‎ובן יקיר אבדתי

I lost. I cried over the death

of the son who was.   לבן פרי חמדתי ‎ל יושב שחקים

the apple of my eyes
To those who dwell in the heavens,

I lift an eye, but I am   אשא עין אריד שיהי‎ ה בצל

cast down.God, in the shadow
of your wings my   כנפיך יחכה נשמתי ורוחי הקדוש
  holy soul and spirit will long for
Naphtali Hertz son of   נפתלי הערץ בר' דוד בראהן נפ'
  Mr. David Brown, died
at age 27 years,   בן כ'ז שנה כ'א תמוז תרע'ח תנצצביה'
  21 Tammuz 5678 (1938)
Let his soul be bound up in
the bonds of the living.

                                             N. H. Brown

Biblical

This epitaph (Temple Beth Abraham, Nashua, New Hampshire) strings together four disparate phrases from the last chapter of the book of Proverbs (also known as *Ei-shet Chayil,* a Woman of Valor,) but organized to spell out the name of the deceased, Brachah, ברכה. Biblical quotes are a common feature of many epitaphs. The most popular source for making acrostics with biblical quotations are Psalm 119 which includes 8 sentences beginning with each letter of the Hebrew alphabet or selected phrases from Proverbs 31:10-31(*Ei-shet Cha-yil*) as shown in the example that follows:

Indeed, the heart of her husband is with her (Prov. 31:11)

בטח בה לב בעלה

Many daughters were made women of valor (Prov. 31:29)

רבות בנות עשוי חיל

She extended her hand to the poor (Prov. 31:20)

כפה פרשה לעני

She was like a storehouse of treasure. (Prov. 31:14 literally: merchant ship)

היתה כאניות סוחר

An Acrostic that's not an Acrostic (Tiffereth Israel of Winthrop, Everett, MA)

The following double headstone is an example of trying to match the format of the two sides of a monument, when one spouse significantly predeceases the other. In this case, the difference was 15 years. The left side is a regular acrostic spelling out the name, *Pesach.* Compare this with the right side. The woman's name, Trina, is spelled out in the right column. However, the letters of her name are not the first letters of the first words of each line. By the way, there is no consistent pattern of which spouse is buried on the left or right.[19]

---

[19] While it is inconsistent, some suggest that the order is man-woman-woman-man, so that a woman is not buried next to a man who was not her husband.

פ"נ

ט	אמנו היקרה	1.
ר	אשה תמימה וישרה	2. פַּאר ראשנו זקן ושבע
יי	אשת חיל עקרת הבית	3. סַתֵר מעשיו צדקה עשה
נ	יראת ה' וחוננת דלים	4. חַסיד ויֹרֹשֹ אבינו היקר
א	ה' טריינא בת ר' צבי	5. רי פסח אליהו
	נפטרה י' חשון תשי"א	6. בֹּ ישראל משה
	תנצב"ה	נפטר כ"ג אדר א' תֹרֹצֹה
		תנצב"ה

Beloved husband and father
Pesach
Died Feb. 26, 1935
Age 80 YRS

Beloved mother
Trina
Died Oct. 21, 1950
Age 83 YRS

GROMAN

Translation:
Here lie

The glory of our old and aged leader:	T	Our beloved mother:
He performed quiet deeds of charity.	R	a perfect and upright woman,
Righteous and God fearing (וִיֹרֹשֹ) was	I	a woman of valor, the
our beloved father,		mistress of her home,
Mr. Pe-sach Ei-li-ya-hu	N	a fearer of God (ה'),
		who favored the
		downtrodden,
son of Mr. Yis-ra-eil Mo-she.	A	the woman (ה'), Trina
		daughter of Mr. Tsvi.
Died 23 A-dar 1 5695		Died 10 Chesh-van 5711
Let his soul...		Let her soul...

Remembering a Beloved Rabbi

Of course, larger monuments offer more spaces for inscriptions. A *ne-fesh* (see chapter 2) in the Sharah Tfilo Section, Baker Street, West Roxbury, MA, contains such a monument to a Rabbi Sprince (1839-1929). It includes four Jewish stars, the hands of the priest and several Biblical quotations. A total of nine inscriptions can be found on the front of this monument. Some are engraved in the stones, while others are attached brass plaques. Rabbi Sprince was born in 1839 and died in 1929. The lengthiest passage on the monument is presented below and is an unusual variation on the acrostic. Most acrostics use only the first letter of each line to spell out a word or name; this inscription uses the first and last letter of each line of the inscription to spell the rabbi's full name, Rabbi She-lo-mo Dov Sprince son of Rabbi Ge-dal-ya-hu the priest, שלמה דוב שפרינץ בהרב גדליהו הכהן. Rabbi Sprince's name and several of his books are shown in larger print on the monument and are shown that way below:

A monument on the grave of	מצבת קבורת
the elderly rabbi and genious.	הרב הגאון הישיש

For 70 years, he was	שבעים שנות מורה צדק ורב
teacher and rabbi	

to different	ל עדות שונות בישראל היה
congregations in Israel.	

90 were the.	מתשעים שנות חיי צדק הגבר
righteous years of the man	

The city of Riga,	העיר ריגא אנשיה אנשי לב
its people, people of understanding,	

clung to him	דבקה בו בראשונה ולראשה הצג
at first and made him leader	

and in the city.	ובעיר בוסתן פנה זיו ההוד
of Boston his glory departed	

134

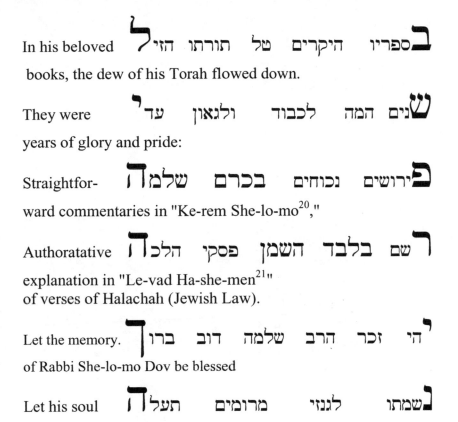

In his beloved   בְּסִפְרִיו הַיְקָרִים טַל תּוֹרָתוֹ הֲזִיל

books, the dew of his Torah flowed down.

They were   שָׁנִים הֵמָּה לְכָבוֹד וּלְגָאוֹן עֲדִי

years of glory and pride:

Straightfor-   פֵּירוּשִׁים נְכוֹחִים בְּכֶרֶם שְׁלֹמֹה

ward commentaries in "Ke-rem She-lo-mo[20],"

Authoratative   רַק שָׁם בִּלְבַד הַשֶּׁמֶן פִּסְקֵי הֲלָכָה

explanation in "Le-vad Ha-she-men[21]"
of verses of Halachah (Jewish Law).

Let the memory.   יְהִי זֵכֶר הָרַב שְׁלֹמֹה דּוֹב בָּרוּךְ

of Rabbi She-lo-mo Dov be blessed

Let his soul   נִשְׁמָתוֹ לְגִנְזֵי מְרוֹמִים תַּעֲלֶה

ascend to the hidden heights.

Let his   צִדְקוֹ וְתוֹרָתוֹ יַלִיצוּ בַּעֲדֵנוּ אָמֵן

righteousness and his Torah intercede for us. Amen.

Poetic Passages

The same themes described above for acrostics, can also be achieved by poetry. The following inscriptions are typical of poetic passages. One problem with poetic passages is that the poetry gets lost in even the best translations.

---

[20] "Vineyard of Solomon": One of Rabbi Sprince's works
[21] "Only the Oil": Another of Rabbi Sprince's works

135

The six lines of poetry also happen to be an acrostic spelling out *Ye-chez-keil* יחזקאל (City of Boston Lodge, Woburn, MA). The first couplet rhyme is "doe", the second is "toe" and the third couple is "hoo." They are underlined.

<u>Translation</u>

Here lies
Our beloved, prominent father   אבינו היקר המופלג
Mr. Yechezkeil (Ezekiel)
    son of Mr. Yosel (Joseph) the Levite   רי יחזקאל בר יוסל הלוי

Fear of God was his substance.   <u>ירא</u> א' היה מעודו
He loved Torah with all his might.   <u>חמד</u> תורה בכל מאודו
The merit of his Torah and righteousness   <u>זכות</u> תורתו וצדקתו
will surely place his his soul first in line.   <u>קדם</u> תקדם פני נשמתו
To dwell in the Temple
 will be his consolation,   <u>אל</u> שוכן מעונה תנחהו
to find refuge in the shadow of His wings.   <u>לחסות</u> בצל כנפיהו
Died on 29 Kislev   נפטר בכ"ט כסלו
year of 5680 (1919), Let his soul...   שנת תריפי תנצצב'ב'ה'
LEVY   לעווי

Another example of a poetic passage occurs on the following following monument for a Physician (Minneapolis Jewish Cemeteries, Penn Ave., Minneapolis, Minnesota,) Abraham Isaac son of Moses, while being a skilled physician, also practiced the values of being a good Jew. He worked to save and preserve life in a Jewish way that stressed his charitability.

Translation		Inscription
Here	Lies	נ פ

An expert physician, a faithful Jew	רופא מומחה, יהודי נאמן
He always believed in being generous.	בנדיבות תמיד האמין
He never shirked his duty.	על טרחתו לא חסה
He was always righteous.	צדקות בכל עת עשה
He cured the	רפה עניים בלי"מ (בלי ממון) התם והכה
poor, the simple and the smitten, without money	
and without	ולשי"ט (ולא שכר טרחה) בכל אתר ואתר זכה
pay in every place	
Abraham Isaac son of Mr. Moses	אברהם אייזיק ב"ר משה
Died 12 Elul 5708 (1948)	נפטר י"ב אלול תש"ח
Let his soul be bound up in the bond of the living	תנצבי'ה'

Prose

The same epitaph themes expressed in acrostics and poetry can also be expressed in prose. Two examples follow. One is very old. The other is recent.

<u>Emphasis on Secular Accomplishments: Joseph Del Medigo</u>
Joseph Del Medigo[22] was a physician and philosopher who lived from 1591 to 1655. His monument is in Prague, Czechoslovakia. The lengthy epitaph is partially prose and partially poetry, but although the son of a rabbi, the grave emphasizes Del Medigo's knowledge of science and secular knowledge.

---

[22] The Jewish Encyclopedia, Volume 12: Entry titled: *Tombstones*, (Funk and Wagnalls, 1906) 192.

Take up weeping, wailing, and lamenting, שאו בכי יללה וקינה וספדו

howl in mourning and desolation, באבילות ובאניה

  suffer bitterness like wormwood, ומרורים שאו כלענה

for a chief and great man has כי נפל שר וגדול במחנה
fallen in the camp,

one who was a crown of אשר היה עטרה

the inherited [i.e. Jewish. לחכמי מורשה ותכונה
learning] and astronomy

Wisdom was lost and נאבדה החכמה ונסתרה התבונה
understanding disappeared.

Is there one like him in clime or country, הנמצא כזה בכל עבר ופינה

  - west, east, south, north - ימה וקדמה נגבה וצפונה

to whom the spirit of אשר רוח אלהים בקרבו נתנה
God has been given?

His wisdom sings in the streets, חכמתו בחוץ תרונה

while his soul, under the wings of נשמתו תחת כנפי

the *Shechinah* (the presense of God), השכינה

  is hidden and preserved. היא גנוזה וטמונה

Hasten, break out in lamentations מהרו וספדו

  and howlings over the man, אוי והוי על גבר

the pride of Israel על גאון ישראל

  who has passed away. אשר בין הגזירה עבר

[Hebrew apparently alludes to Abraham's experience in Genesis 15:17]

For he is Joseph who sold corn כי הוא זה יוסף המשביר בר
(cf. Genesis 42:6),

whose reputation spread everywhere, אשר שמעו הולך בכל עבר

who tore up the mountains and broke rocks. מפרק הרים וסלעים שבר

Nothing was hidden from him. ולא נעלם ממנו

In language that speaks great things, כל דבר בלשון מדברת גדולות

he composed works. ספרים חבר

In the book "*Noblot* ספר נובלות החכמה נכבדות

Ha-Choch-mah Nich-ba-dot[23]"

he credibly speaks	בהם מדבר בתכונה
of astronomy and calendar calculations.	כפשוטה ועיבור
To compose many works	לעשות ספרים הרבה
was his intention and his desire.	גמר וסבר
In all the seven sciences	ובכל שבע חכמות היה כגובר גבר
he was very efficient.	
He omitted nothing, small or great;	לא הניח דבר קטן וגדול
he collected and Thesaurized all.	חבל אסף וצבר

A Rhode Island Banker

Another example of a prose epitaph is taken from the Old
Colonial Jewish Cemetery, Newport, Rhode Island. The
monument of Moses Seixas indicates that his interests were
generally in business and civics beyond the scope of the Jewish
Community. The epitaph also shows that monuments with
minimal Hebrew are not a recent change.

1. (Monument of)	מצבת
2.	Moses Seixas
3.	died 4th Chisleu[24] 5570,
4.	being Nov. 29, 1809
5.	Aged 66,
6.	He was Grand Master of the
7.	Grand Lodge of the Masonic
8.	order of this State & Cashier of
9.	The Bank of Rhode Island from its
10.	commencement to his death

---

[23] Ibid. The Jewish Encyclopedia: Note, there is a lengthy Bibliography of
Del Medigo in the article. However, the article merely transliterated this
title. Perhaps the author did so because he was unsure of the meaning: A
possible meaning based on Del Medigo's life could be "Honorable Secular
Knowledge".

[24] The transliteration of the Hebrew month, כסלו, is usually Kislev or
Kisleiv. "Chisleu" is either very unusual or an error.

Military Monuments

Jews take great pride in their contributions to the countries in which they live. The following monument, that of Jacob Scharf שארף (Austrian Cemetery Association, Woburn, MA), is an example of carrying patriotism right to the grave and ultimately the monument at the grave. In addition to the Hebrew, we learn more about his commitment from an additional English inscription, which is also included below.

Translation
  Here lies

פ׳ ✡ נ׳

our beloved son,	בננו היקר
the young man,	הבחור
Jacob	יעקב
son of Mr.	בר׳
Ze-eiv Wolf (William)	זאב וואלף
Born 14 Shevat	נולד יד שבט
in the year 5659 (1899)	שנת תרנט
and died 4 Nisan	וני ד ניסן
in the year of 5678 (1918)	שנת תרעח
He gave his life for	נפשו מסר בעד
his country, the United States	ארצו ארי הברית
and he died like a hero	ונפל כגבור
in the field of battle	בשדה המלחמה
in the country of France.	במדינת צרפת

One of the first
to serve his contry(sic)
and the first
to give his life
in the
Great World War
from Everett Mass.

140

A trip through a cemetery will show a disproportionately large number of monuments describing the deceased's participation in the armed services. These monuments include name, branch(es) of service, year of birth, year of death. In addition they also may include military rank, war service, day and dates of birth and death, a Jewish star; valor awards and Purple Hearts. Terms of endearment such as "Our beloved ...", nicknames, significant accomplishments and titles such as "Doctor" may also be included. The United States Veteran's Administration explains that these are provided free-of-charge to any veteran or spouse of a veteran, unless the veteran received a dishonorable discharge. These monuments come in the following three styles:

1. Upright white marble or light gray granite, 42" x 13" x 4"
2. Flat white marble or light gray granite, 24" x 12" x 4"
3. Bronze 24" x 12" x 0.75"

10. Epitaphs of General Interest

This chapter is a summary of a number of miscellaneous items provided on monuments. It is the occasional find of an inscription like these that keeps me looking for interesting cemetery inscriptions. In the movie, "Forrest Gump," Forrest quotes his mother as having said, "Life is like a box of chocolates. You never know what you're gonna get." In some ways, the same is true of a cemetery visit. Most of the monuments will be ordinary, but every so often, one appears that is quite special. With that in mind, the material in this chapter is in no particular order, which should give a potential cemetery visitor an opportunity to experience things the way they appear in cemeteries: randomly and out of context.

Cause of Death

If the cause of death is a war, it is often mentioned in Hebrew, English or (see Chapter 9 regarding military monuments.) Otherwise, the cause of death is rarely given. Through great flu epidemics, notably in 1918 and 1919, there are references to people dying (in the prime of life) but not the cause. The following epitaphs and phrases actually suggest the cause of death.

Ambush in war: (Manchester, NH)

| On a convoy | Al shai-ye-rah | עַל שׁירה |
| that was massacred | ha ka-tal | הקטל |

Childbirth: (Montifiore, Woburn, MA)

She died in childbirth   va-te-kash be-li-da-tah   ותקש בלדתה
[Literally: She had a difficult labor (cf. Gen. 35:16 - Death of Rachel)]

Fire: (Chelsea Chevra Kaddisha, Woburn, MA)

From the heights	Mi-ma-rom	ממרום
He (God) sent fire.	sha-lach eish	שלח אש
(Lam. 1:13)		

143

Illness: (Chelsea Chevra Kaddisha, Woburn, MA)

| Sickness overtook | Ma-cha-leh av-ra | מחלה עברה |
| your soul. | naf-she-cha | נפשך |

Lightning: (Cong. Ahavat Shalom, Lynn, No. Reading, MA)

The lightning flashed,	Hei-ir ba-rak	האיר ברק
thunder did roar,	Nish-ma ra-am	נשמע רעם
and the heart ,	ve-leiv	ולב העלם
of the young man,	ha-e-lem	
would beat no more.	cha-dal le-fa-am.	חדל לפעם

Murder during an armed robbery: (Beth Joseph 1, Woburn, MA)

| He was laid lifeless (cf. Ju. 5:27) | Na-fal sha-dud | נפל שדוד |
| by the hands of a murderer | bi-dei me-ra-tsei-ach | בידי מרצח |

The Common death of twins (Netherlands Cemetery, Melrose, MA)

One can only imagine the pain of the parents, at the loss of one child, but with twins, it is two. Consider the following inscription:

Behold, there were twins in her womb   והנה תאומים בבטנה

The Hebrew of Genesis 25:24 reads: והנה תומים בבטנה. The Hebrew of Genesis 38:27 reads: והנה תאומים בבטנה. The Hebrew on the monument is that of Genesis 38:27.

Genesis 25:24 refers to Rebecca giving birth to Jacob and Esau. Genesis 38:27 is the result of the seduction of Judah by Tamar and the children are Peretz and Zerach. Was this an error? Was the text really intended to refer to Jacob and Esau? Perhaps the person checking the monument added the aleph intentionally. The thinking might have been that he did not want to associate the survival of Judaism through Jacob, with a set of twins who did not survive childbirth.

144

Or perhaps it was no mistake at all and the choice of the Genesis 38:27 passage was done intentionally to reflect Rashi's (a medieval commentator) understanding that the twins, Peretz and Zerach, were equal; but Jacob and Esau were not.

Zebras and doctors

A common expression among physicians is "If you hear hoofbeats, expect horses, not zebras." The expression usually means "don't look for an extraordinary solution until the standard ones have been exhausted."

Next to the new Beit Olam Cemetery in Wayland, MA is a small section of the "Town of Wayland's North Cemetery". In it is a grouping of perhaps 30 Jewish graves. The grave of one physician gave the man's name only in English and his year of birth and year of death. Immediately below was the following Hebrew inscription:

<u>Translation</u>

Just because you hear the sound of galloping	כשתשמע קול דחירת (sic דהירה)
don't. expect to see a zebra	אל תצפות (תצפה sic) לראות זברח (זברה sic)

Many quotes from the Bible, the Talmud and the liturgy are translated into English. This inscription is unusual in that it

145

translates a common English expression into Hebrew. But independent of that, what message is being given?

Was this just an expression that the deceased physician used routinely, so his survivors placed it as a reminder of these words of wisdom? Was there some measure of irony in that the doctor passed away from something obscure because they looked at the simple, or vice verse? Or was it something completely different?

Play on Words associated with the Date

Sometimes, the year of death also spells out a word. One negative example noted in Chapter 7, was 5744, תשמ"ד, meaning "destruction" which is often rewritten תשד"מ.

The year was 5650 (1890CE), which is תר"ן in Hebrew letters. To-ren (תרן) means "mast", but in this context, it meant "monument" (from Ouderkerk, Netherlands).

This monument was chiseled in the year 5650,	תרן זה חצב בשנת תרן
a monument forever to the importance of the man	תרן לעד חשבות האיש
who lies beneath it.	המנח תחתיו

A child named Jacob: יעקב. (Beth Joseph 2, Woburn, MA)

Sometimes a mere allusion to the weekly Torah reading can give a lengthy message in a mere two words. Suppose for a moment that the monument read:

Born in the week when Gen. 37(Va-yei-shev) was read	נולד פ' וישב
	...
Died on the Sabbath when Gen. 12 (Lech Le-cha) was read.	ויעל לשמים שבת קדש פ' לך לך

146

If this were the case, the two Torah portions give the entire message that God gives and God takes away.

On Jacob's birth, he moved into his father's house:
Genesis 37:1: And Jacob settled in the land where his father had resided, ...

And on Jacob's death, he departed his father's house:
Genesis 12:1: God said, "... Go forth ... from your father's house to the land that I (God) will show you."

This might be the end of the story, except that's not what the monument says! What it really says is:

Born in the week when Gen. 30 (Va-yish-lach) was read   נולד פ׳ וישלח

This would have been the correct Torah reading for the previous week which corresponded to the last section of the Torah read prior to Jacobs birth. Was this a mistake or was this a third part of the message?
Genesis 30:1 "And Jacob sent messengers in front of him..."

If it is the third part of the message, we now understand that Jacob checked out the future (30:1), Jacob moved in with his earthly family (37:1), Jacob returned to God (12:1).

Erected by his daughter ... (Anshe Lebovitz, Woburn, MA)
The monument discussed next is a standard mix of Hebrew and English. As a result, its contents are not included here. However, at the bottom of the monument is the inscription, "Erected by his daughter ... ." and at the top the same statement is inscribed in Yiddish.
[ערעטער באי ... ... זיין טאכטער].

Monument inscriptions don't generally refer to the actions of the living. Perhaps her father was a difficult person who was known not to get along with his daughter. Was this statement made by her to quell gossip and to let others know that she had made peace with her father?

Perhaps this line is a reference to a family feud. Was there a brother or other siblings who were unwilling to share the expenses?

A Bride named Hessie האסי (Woburn, MA)
This inscription is amazing. What are the odds of a bride dying on the date of her wedding? Based on the time, the odds are good that she was a victim of a flu epidemic.

<u>Translation</u>

פ'נ'

Here lies
our beloved daughter, the bride
Hessie daughter of
  Menachem Nachum
died in the prime of her life
on her wedding day
20 Tevet 5679
Let her soul....

בתנו הכלה היקרה
האסי בת ר' מנחם נחום

נפטרה בדמי ימיה
ביום המעד לכלולותיה
כ טבת תרעט
תנצביה'

Our darling
daughter and sister
Katherine Matross
Died on the day of
her wedding
December 23, 1918

148

Where

Many monuments include place names where a person was born or where he/she died. Chapter 2 discussed the importance that Jews assign to ownership of burial plots. However, this one leaves me asking, "If I didn't know where this monument was, how would I find it. And if I did, what new information is this inscription giving me?" Regardless, the following made it clear exactly where in the cemetery the viewer was standing. (Chelsea Chevra Kadisha, Woburn, MA.)

Buried in row 2, position 18   נקברה בשורה ב", נ" 18

11. Monument Fabrication and Errors

This chapter deals with the fabrication process of monuments and monument inscriptions, but the bulk of the chapter is about the huge variety of possible and actual errors.

Fabrication

The majority of monuments are stones, but an increasing percentage of more modern monuments use brass plaques. One reason for this is that brass plaques cost considerably less than stones.

Since most monument manufacturers do not know Hebrew, stones or brass plaques are generally laid out on a mask using a lettering chart in which each Hebrew letter is numbered.

Example:

1	2	3	4	5	6	7	8	9	10	11	12 ...
א	ב	ג	ד	ה	ו	ז	ח	ט	י	כ	ך ...

To have the name, Tuviah (טוביה), inscribed in Hebrew, the following data would be supplied to the monument maker:

5 10 2 6 9

After the mask is made, the most common way to add the lettering to the stone is by sandblasting. Brass plaques are etched.

Errors

Mistakes are common in the fabrication process. Often, the person who supplies the list of numbers to make the mask, or the person who transcribes the letters to the mask makes an error.

Those who are careful will double-check the masks before the monument is completed, but mistakes still occur. In some cases, especially in small outlying communities, it is clear that no one is available to check the Hebrew spellings. Sometimes the method for generating the Hebrew is to copy a pre-existing monument. The net effect is that many of the later monuments duplicate the mistakes of the earlier ones.

Once a mistake is made, it can be fixed. The following example shows that the "NOV" date of birth was erroneously put on the monument and it was later corrected to "JAN". The mistake looks good at the unveiling of the monument. This photo was taken about after 25 years after the monument was erected. Wear and erosion took its toll.

What follows are categories of errors with actual examples.

Grammar (noun adjective agreement):

Actual:	Correct:
אמנו יקרה	אמנו היקרה
I-mei-nu ye-ka-ra	I-mei-nu ha-ye-ka-ra
	Our beloved mother

The following epitaph (Chevra Kaddisha of Chelsea, Woburn, MA) is an example where the author chose correct poetry over correct grammar. The rhyme in the transliteration is underlined.

... the body of a	...ge-vi-at	...גוית
beloved spiritual man.	ish ya-kar ru-ach	איש יקר רוח
Truth and righteousness	Ha-e-met ve-ha-tse-dek	האמת והצדק
rest with him.	i-mo ta-nu-ach	עמו תנוח

Ya-nu-chu (ינוחו) would more correctly reflect the plural of "truth and righteousness" rather than *ta-nu-ach* (תנוח) which reflects only the feminine noun, truth (אמת).

Spelling

Spelling errors can sometimes occur. The following is an example of both an omission and an incorrect letter on the same Biblical quote observed at Framingham-Natick Jewish Cemeteries, Natick, MA:

Actual: אַנִי לדודי ודוי לי   חַנִי לדודי ודוי לי   Correct: אַנִי לדוּדַי לִי

Transliteration: *A-ni le-do-di ve-do-di li.*
Translation: I am my beloved's and my beloved is mine.
[Song of Songs 6:3.]

The above is an example where the errors were incidental. The following is an example where the omission of a single Hebrew letter surely changes the perspective (Independent Gold Crown, Woburn, MA)! Note, that in the English part of the inscription, it does say, "Dear wife."

Translation of the Error	Error	Translation	Correct
a frigid wife	אשה קרה	beloved wife	אשה יקרה

Metathesis

Sometimes two letters have their order switched by any number of methods ranging from dyslexia to working too

153

quickly. The example shown below from Roxbury Mutual, Woburn, MA, underlines the word in question.

Correct Translation	As it appeared on the stone	As it should have been
Cha-ya daughter of ...	חיה תב אריה לייב	חיה בת אריה לייב

Errors: Look Alike Letters

Mistakes can sometimes be a result of look-alike letters. The following is a list of look-alike letters:

יוזן	זך	דרך	בכ	סם
טמ	עצ	גנו	החת	

Multi-letter look alikes:

מ כו   מ כז

Actual examples (error underlined):

Translation of the Error	Error	Translation	Correct
Your farmer	אכַרך (*I-kar-chah*)	Young man (*Av-reich*)	אברך
In her mouth	בפיה	Her palm	כפיה
With a pig	בחזר	Lad or young man	בחור
200th of Adar	ר אדר	4th of Adar	ד אדר

(Note: On the above, the Gregorian date was given which confirmed that this was not an abbreviation for "Rosh Chodesh".)

verily	אמנן	Our mother	אמנו
40th of Ta-muz	מ תמוז	26 Ta-muz	כו תמוז
-	יעחק	Isaac	יצחק
my whore	זונתי	my mate (or wife)	זונתי

Note: This error can be found in the back of the Crawford Street Shul Cemetery, Baker St., W. Roxbury, MA on the monument of a woman who died in 1937. The mistake in the Hebrew is somewhere between amusing and outrageous. It is shown below in order to be believed!

Errors: Final Letters

There are 22 distinct letters in Hebrew. In addition, 5 letters have forms that are used only when they occur at the end of a word. They are:

כ ך   מ ם   נ ן   פ ף   צ ץ

Sometimes the final letters are misused as the following example shows:

Actual example (error underlined):

	Error	Translation	Correct
	מרימ	Miriam	מרים

Also, each Hebrew letter has a numeric value. The final letters theoretically represent the larger numbers, 500 through 900 as described in Chapter 7. In reality, final letters are not generally used as numbers on monuments. Their use at the end of a number is one of the most common errors one might see. Example: 5720 represented as תש"ך rather than תש"כ. The mistake is so common that some might argue it is not a mistake but common usage.

Errors: Sound Alike Letters

Mistakes can also be a result of "sound alike" letters. The following is a list of the most common "sound alike" errors.

אע   אה (Both silent at the end of a word.)   בו

זצ   חכך   טת   כק   ססת

Actual examples (error underlined):

Error	Translation	Correct
עֲלִיהו	Elijah	אליהו
כסלֵב	Kislev (Name of month)	כסלו
היכַרה	Beloved	היקרה
נצֵך	Forever	נצח

Errors: Multiple Part Letters

Another type of error is the omission of a piece of a "*hei*" or "*kuf*" which complicates the decoding of an inscription. The "*kuf*" to "*kaf*" error is also discussed above as a "sound alike letter error". If the inscription is not badly weathered, one can distinguish between the shape of the "*kaf*" and the right half of the "*kuf*".

ה as ר or ד   ק as כ or ב

Actual Examples (error underlined):

Error	Translation	Correct
יכַר	Beloved	יקר
ריקרה	Beloved	היקרה

Errors: Dots, Vowels and Punctuation

Dots as vowels and punctuation are not generally used. Occasionally, someone will use a dot in the following letters: ה, פ, כ or ב. Most other marks that appear to be punctuation or vowels are usually indicators of abbreviations. These include single quotes, double quotes, dots and tildes.

Certain Hebrew letters are used as vowels. These include *alef*, *hei*, *vav* and *yod*. *Vav*s are sometimes doubled to indicate consonantal *vav*s. *Yod*s are sometimes doubled to indicate a long "a" vowel. Single *yod*s are sometimes added to indicate a long "i" vowel.

Sometimes, however, extra letters are added as errors. One common error is on the word meaning "our mother." This error arises because "our father," is correctly written in Hebrew as "avinu" אבינו. "Our mother," however, is correctly written in Hebrew as "imeinu" אמנו. Sometimes "our mother" is carelessly entered as אמינו, erroneously using אבינו as the paradigm.

Errors: Dates and Years

Errors on a monument can occur when computing the Hebrew date of a person's death. One can compute the Hebrew year by adding 3760 to the common (Christian) year on the monument, if the death was between January 1 and the day prior to Rosh Hashannah. If the date was between Rosh Hashannah and December 31, the number to add is 3761. Detailed methods were provided both in chapters 3 and 7 for this computation.

Another common error might be a one-day difference between the date of death on the common calendar and the date on the Hebrew calendar. This is due to the fact that the common calendar moves to the next date at midnight, while the Hebrew calendar moves to the next date at sunset (nominally 6 PM). An example: a monument indicated that the person memorialized died on the first day Rosh Chodesh Iyar, 5712 (i.e. the 30th of Nisan). The common date on the monument for the date of death was April 24, 1952. In fact April 24, 1952 was the 29th of Nisan until sunset.

Errors: Spacing

Sometimes, words are not properly spaced. This creates a special challenge to those decoding the contents of the monument. Not only do the decoders have to figure out the meaning of the words, they have to figure out where one word ends and the next one begins.

Here is one such example (from the Elmwood Cemetery, Great Barrington, MA).

ד"אבתשמ"ד

After staring at it for a while, it parses to:
ד"י אב תשמ"ד, merely: the 4th of Av 5744.

Errors: Omissions and Ambiguities
The following graphic, which combines an aleph and a la-

med, , is often used as a substitute for אל. However, frequently, letters are omitted. On older monuments, line lengths were poorly planned, so squeezing letters together or letter omissions at the end of lines were not so much a result of poor editing as poor planning.

Monuments are replete with abbreviations which lead to ambiguity. A tool to help is *A Treasury of Acronyms* אוצר[25] ראשי תבות which has approximately 600 pages of abbreviations from the Talmud and Jewish literature. Adding to the confusion is the fact that the same abbreviation or acronym can mean something different, depending on where on the monument it occurs.

Calendar software programs can check the more obvious omissions in dates, because most monuments have both the Hebrew calendar dates and the common calendar dates on them.

[25] Ashkenai, Shmueil and Yardein, Dov, אוצר ראשי תבות, [A Treasury of Acronyms] (Rubin Mass, Jerusalem, Israel, 1978)

One example of this kind of ambiguity is shown in a date on a monument that stated the date of death was "2nd day of New Moon, 5688." Depending on the year, this could have been any of as many as 8 of the months. A look at the calendar for 5688 showed 7 possible months, but once the common calendar date was factored in, only one month was possible.

Error: Upside Down Inscription/Mirror Image
A careful look at the decoration in the monument shown below will show the letters פ"נ in the center of the Magen David. These letters are shown in mirror image, probably because the Magen David decoration became separated from the rest of the mask. The monument was observed in Beth Joseph 2, Woburn, MA.

God Repairs
The following story was related to me. The teller told me I could use it, as long as I didn't mention him by name.

> My late father-in-law was a very difficult person, to say the least. Never physically abusive, and having a low self-esteem, he was verbally abusive in ways that permanently scarred his wife and children.
>
> On a recent visit to the cemetery it was evident that providence is ever at work. Bird droppings on his monument

had all but totally obliterated the word "beloved" from the inscription, "beloved husband and father."

Just as erosion exposes mistakes, a pigeon became God's agent to amend accordingly.

Shibboleths, Inside Information and Local Accents
There are things written on monuments that reflect local idioms and insider information. Without knowing the stories, some of these can be undecodable even to someone fluent in Hebrew.

Sometimes, the challenge isn't the Hebrew, but the decoration. On the monument of a 93 year old woman (Montifiore, Woburn, MA) who died in 1994 is the name, Eva "Bubba" Wiseman. The monument is shown below.

Her date of birth and death were inscribed directly below. Her Hebrew name and Hebrew date of death just above. In the upper left corner is a floral pattern and between her common calendar day of birth and death is a candelabrum. "Bubba" means grandma in Yiddish. (However, in 1990's English, that specific spelling has a redneck implication associated with it.)

But in the upper right hand corner, shown in a blow-up next to the monument, is a beer can with the word "Budweiser" inscribed on it. Maybe this was a pun: Bubba Wiseman = Bud Weiser? Maybe the family was reflecting on some aspect of her life that gave her joy, namely Budweiser Beer. Maybe beer became a humorous footnote to her life in her dotage.

But as a casual passerby, I was unable to understand. The bottom line: be careful of what is put on a monument. It will be there, long after the insiders who understand have also passed away.

Error: I'm all mixed up
The following footstone (Adath Israel, Massena, NY) has errors that defy categorization!

1. Here lies	פ"נ
2. On the 22nd day of Tei-veit Tsvi,	ביום כ"ב טבת צבי
3. Mr. Israel son of Mr. 5706	ר ישראל ב"ר תש"ו

EDWARD I. GLICKMAN
AGE 67 DIED DEC. 26, 1945

Let his soul be bound up in the bonds of the living.   תנצ'ב'ה'

As you can see, all the information is there. It's just in the wrong order! The conclusion is that Edward Glickman's monument should have read as follows and how lines 2 and 3 got mixed up, anybody's guess:

1. Here lies	פ"נ
3. Mr. Israel son of Mr. 2.Tsvi,	ר ישראל ב"ר צבי
2. (Died) On the 22nd day of Tei-veit 3. 5706	(נפ') ביום כ"ב טבת תש"ו

12. Sample Monument Inscriptions

Before visiting a cemetery, use this section to try your knowledge of monuments. Using the information contained in this book, fill in the blanks in the following examples of monuments. If you get stuck, the solutions are in the back of the chapter. Unless marked otherwise, the inscriptions should be decodable by using Chapter 3.

#1:

פ"נ

FATHER

אבינו היקר

ר' אפרים יוסף

בן ר' משה

נפ' כ"ג כסלו תשי"ב

תנצב"ה

FRANK Mondlick Dec. 21, 1951

1. פ <decoration: _____> נ'
    Likely options: Magen David, Menorah, Hands

2. Introductory Line _____

3. Name _____

4. Date of death   Year   Month   Day
   נפ' _____|_____|_____

5. Epitaph

   or צ"ל or ז"ל or תנצב"ה

   _____

163

#2:

פ"נ

אמנו היקרה

שרה בת ר' מרדכי הלוי

נפ' יז' אייר תרצ"ה

תנצב"ה

Died May 20, 1935

Sarah Berger

1.   נ' <decoration: _____> פ'

       Likely options: Magen David, Menorah, Hands

2. Introductory Line   _____

3. Name   _____

4. Date of death   Year   Month   Day

    _____|_____|_____ 'נפ

5. Epitaph

תנצב"ה or ז"ל or זצ"ל or

_____

#3: Lines 2 and 4 of this monument may provide a challenge.

פ'נ' ✡

Line 1:
Line 2:   האיש הישר
Line 3:   יצחק בן עשו
Line 4:   רייננאלד
Line 5:   נפ' כ"ח תמוז היתשמב
Line 6:   תניצב"ה'
                                                                July 16, 1982

----

1.   נ' <decoration: _____> פ'
          Likely options: Magen David, Menorah, Hands

2. Introductory Line   _____

3. Name   _____

4. Date of death   Year   Month   Day
                        _____|_____|_____ נפ'

5. Epitaph

          תניצב"ה' or ז"ל or זצ"ל or _____

          _____

#4: This inscription is a little more difficult because of the word grouping. The conventional grouping described in Chapter 3 is shown at the bottom of this page. The other complicating factor is the date of death is given as a holiday rather than as a calendar date.

Line 1:	פנ
Line 2:	האשה הצנועה
Line 3:	מר"ת שרה מלכה
Line 4:	בת משה שהלכה
Line 5:	לעולמה ביום
Line 6:	הכפורים שנת
Line 7:	תרעח לפ"ק
	Sept. 26, 1917

Alternate Grouping of lines:

פנ

האשה הצנועה

מר"ת שרה מלכה בת משה

שהלכה לעולמה ביום הכפורים שנת תרעח לפ"ק

Sept. 26, 1917

1.   נ' <decoration: _____> פ'

     Likely options: Magen David, Menorah, Hands

2. Introductory Line   _____

3. Name   _____

4. Date of death   Year   Month   Day

                           נפ' _____|_____|_____

5. Epitaph

     or תניצביה or זיל or זציל

_____

#5:

Line 1:	פ"נ
Line 2:	אבינו היקר המופלג
Line 3:	ר' יעקב בר' ארי צבי
Line 4:	שווארץ
Line 5:	נפטר כ"ט סיון תרפ"ד
Line 6:	תנצב"ה

Jacob Schwartz
July 1, 1924

1.   נ' <decoration: _____> פ'

Likely options: Magen David, Menorah, Hands

2. Introductory Line   _____

3. Name   _____

4. Date of death   Year   Month   Day

נפ' _____|_____|_____

5. Epitaph

or תנצב"ה or ז"ל or זצ"ל

_____

#6: The following example shows how this 1829 headstone, in Lublin, Poland reflects language very similar to what one might see today[26].

Example

Line 1:	נפטר יג אב תקפט לפק
Line 2:	<books>
Line 3:	פ"נ איש נבון וחכם
Line 4:	תם וישר וירא אלקים
Line 5:	והגה תורת ה' לילות וימי'
Line 6:	זקן ושבע ימים ה"ה
Line 7:	איש צדיק תמים הרבני
Line 8:	מ' ברוך יעקב בן מו"ה
Line 9:	אברהם שלמה ז"ל

1. Date of death   Year   Month   Day

נפ' _____|_____|_____

2: decoration: Books

3. Introductory Line(cont.) _____

4. Introductory Line(cont.) _____

5. Introductory Line(cont.) _____

6. Introductory Line(cont.) _____

7. Introductory Line(cont.) _____

8. Name   _____

9. Name (cont.)   _____

9(cont.). Epitaph

תנצב"ה or ז"ל or זצ"ל or _____

---

[26] Vishniac, R., *Polish Jews* (Schocken, NY, 1976), 31

<u>Solution to Example #1</u>

Line 1:   פ"נ

                                     FATHER

Line 2:   אבינו היקר

Line 3:   ר' אפרים יוסף

Line 3(cont.)   בן ר' משה

Line 4:   נפ' כ"ג כסלו תשי"ב

Line 5:   תנצב"ה

                                  FRANK Mondlick
                                 Died Dec. 21, 1951

Line 1: Decoration   No Decoration: Here lies
Line 2: Introductory Line   Our beloved father
Line 3: Name   Mr. Ef-ra-yim Yo-seiph
Line 3: (cont.)   son of Mr. Mo-she
Line 4: Date   Died 23rd of Kislev 5712
Line 5: Epitaph Let his soul be bound up in the bonds of the living.

<u>Solution to Example #2</u>

Line 1:   פ"נ

Line 2:   אמנו היקרה

Line 3:   שרה בת ר' מרדכי הלוי

Line 4:   נפ' י"ז אייר תרצ"ה

Line 5:   תנצב"ה

                                 Died May 20, 1935
                                   Sarah Berger

Line 1: Decoration   No Decoration: Here lies
Line 2: Introductory Line   Our beloved mother
Line 3: Name   Sarah daughter of Mr. Mordechai the Levite
Line 4: Date   Died 17th of Iyar 5695
Line 5: Epitaph Let her soul be bound up in the bonds of the living.

169

Solution to Example #3
Line 1: Decoration

פ׳ ✡ נ׳

Line 2: Introductory Line	האיש הישר
Line 3: Name	יצחק בן עשו
Line 4: Surname	ריינגאלד
Line 5: Date	נפ׳ כ״ח תמוז היתשמב
Line 6: Epitaph	תנצ׳ב׳ה׳

Isaac Reingold
July 16, 1982

Line 1: Here <Decoration: Magen David> lies
Line 2: the upright man
Line 3: Isaac son of Esau[27]
Line 4: Reingold
Line 5: Died 28th of Ta-muz 5742
Line 6: Let his soul be bound up in the bonds of the living.

---

[27] Certain names are unusual as Jewish names. For example, post-Holocaust, "Adolph" disappeared. "Esau" is very unusual as a Jewish name and I suspect that the name may well have been "Issa" or any number of other Yiddish diminutives and its spelling as עשו is an error.

Solution to Example #4

Line 1: Decoration   פנ

Line 2: Introductory Line   האשה הצנועה

Line 3: Name   מר"ת שרה מלכה

Line 4: Name + start of date   בת משה שהלכה

Line 5: Date continues   לעולמה ביום

Line 6: Date continues   הכפורים שנת

Line 7: Date concludes   תרעח לפ"ק

                                 Sept. 26, 1917

Line 1: Here lies

Line 2: the humble woman

Line 3: Mrs. Sarah Malcah

Line 4: daughter of Moses who went

Line 5: to her world (i.e. died) on the Day

Line 6: of Atonement, in the year of

Line 7: 5678 by the Jewish calendar.

The conventional grouping described in Chapter 3 is shown below.

Here lies   פנ

Classic Introductory line   האשה הצנועה

Name: \<Title\>\<name\>   מר"ת שרה מלכה בת משה

  \<daughter of\>\<father's name\>

Date:\<Died\>\<holiday\>\<year\>

       שהלכה לעולמה ביום הכפורים שנת תרעח לפ"ק

171

Line 1: Decoration   פ"נ

Line 2: Introductory Line   אבינו היקר המופלג

Line 3: Name   ר' יעקב בר' ארי צבי

Line 4: Surname   שווארץ

Line 5: Date   נפטר כ"ט סיון תרפ"ד

Line 6: Epitaph   תנצב"ה

Jacob Schwartz

July 1, 1924

Line 1: Here lies

Line 2: our beloved and prominent father

Line 3: Mr. Jacob son of Mr. Ari Tsvi

Line 4: Schwartz

Line 5: Died 29th of Sivan 5684

Line 6: Let his soul be bound up in the bonds of the living.

Solution to Example #6

Line 1:   נפטר יג אב תקפט לפק

Line 2:   <books>

Line 3:   פ"נ איש נבון וחכם

Line 4:   תם וישר וירא אלקים

Line 5:   והגה תורת ה' לילות וימי'

Line 6:   זקן ושבע ימים ה"ה

Line 7:   איש צדיק תמים הרבני

Line 8:   מ' ברוך יעקב בן מו'ה

Line 9:   אברהם שלמה ז"ל

Line 1: Date: Died 13th of Av 5589 by the Jewish calendar (1829 C.E.). The key clue to the above line as the "date line" is given by the opening word, נפטר.

Line 2: Decoration<books>: Books are indicative that the man was a scholar.

Line 3: Introductory Line: Here lies a sage and a wise man.
Line 3 is either the "Introductory Line" or the "name line". The opening letters, פ"נ, gives the key clue. When what follows is clearly not a name, we conclude that this is the "Introductory Line" rather than the "name line".

Line 4: Introductory Line (cont.): perfect and honest and feared God

Line 5: Introductory Line (cont.): and studied the Torah of God nights and his days

Line 6: Introductory Line (cont.): old and full of days, ה"ה
Note: ה"ה is extremely generic, with the possibility of almost any noun and any adjective. Suggested possibilities, given the context, could be any of the following:
The honored sir האדון הנכבד; The great sage החכם הגדול; The great Rabbi הרב הגדול

Line 7: Introductory Line (cont.): A righteous and perfect man, the Rabbi
Note: The "Introductory line" transitions to the "name line". The clue is the title, מ' in line 8.

Line 8: Name: Mr. Ba-ruch Ya-a-kov son of our Rabbi and teacher

Line 9: Name continue and Epitaph: Av-ra-ham She-lo-mo of blessed memory
The epitaph is only the ז"ל half of line 9.

Appendix A. Holiday Differences for Jews Living in Israel and Reform Jews

The holiday dates listed in this appendix are designed to help you understand variations and differences on cemetery monuments. It is important to notice that most Jews living in the diaspora (outside of Israel) celebrate an extra day to the holidays of Passover, Shavuot and Sukkot which are known collectively as "the three festivals." Each of the three festivals is celebrated for one less day by Reform Jews and by Israelis. For example, Passover is commemorated for 7 days by Reform and Israeli Jews. The first day of the holiday is *chag* (i.e. full holiday status), which is followed by 5 intermediate days, and ends with one day of *chag*. For Orthodox and Conservative Jews in the diaspora, Passover lasts for eight days with the first two days as *chag*, followed by 4 intermediate days, and ending with two days of *chag*.

For Reform Jews and by Israelis, Sukkot is commemorated for 8 days. The first day is *chag* (i.e. full holiday status), followed by 6 intermediate days and ending with one day of *chag*. For non-Reform diaspora Jews, Sukkot is celebrated for 9 days, where the first two days are *chag*, followed by 5 intermediate days and ending with two days of *chag*.

Shavuot in Israel and for Reform Jews is merely one day instead of two.

Table of Holiday Designations for Israelis and Reform Jews

Passover	Pesach (15 Nisan)	פסח	פ'
Day before Passover	14 Nisan	ערב [ד]פסח	ע[ד]פ'
1st day	15 Nisan	א [ד]פסח	א [ד]פ'
2nd day	16 Nisan	א [ד]חול המועד פסח	א [ד]חהפ'
3rd day	17 Nisan	ב [ד]חול המועד פסח	ב [ד]חהפ'
4th day	18 Nisan	ג [ד]חול המועד פסח	ג [ד]חהפ'
5th day	19 Nisan	ד [ד]חול המועד פסח	ד [ד]חהפ'

6th day	20 Nisan	ה]ד[חול המועד פסח	ה]ד[חהפ'
7th day	21 Nisan	ז]ד[פסח	ז]ד[פ'
Last day of Passover	21 Nisan	יום אחרון]ד[פסח	

22 Nisan (after sunset, before midnight) Mo-tsei Pe-sach מוצאי פסח

| First day after Passover | Is-ru Chag Pesach 22 Nisan | אסרו חג]ד[פסח | אח'ן]ד[פ |

<u>Feast of Weeks</u>   <u>Shavuot (6 Sivan)</u>   שבועות

| Day before Shavuot | 5 Sivan | ערב]ד[שבועות | ע]ד[ש |
| 1st day | 6 Sivan | א]ד[שבועות | |

6 Sivan (after sunset, before midnight) מוצאי שבועות

| First day after Shavuot | Is-ru Chag Shavuot 7 Sivan | אסרו חג]ד[שבועות | אח']ד[ש |

<u>Feast of Tabernacles</u>   <u>Sukkot(15 Tishri)</u>סכות or סוכות

Eve of Sukkot	14 Tishri	ערב]ד[דסוכות	ע]ד[ס'
1st day	15 Tishri	א]ד[סוכות	א]ד[ס'
2nd day	16 Tishri	א]ד[חול המועד סוכות	א]ד[חהס'
3rd day	17 Tishri	ב]ד[חול המועד סוכות	ב]ד[חהס'
4th day	18 Tishri	ג]ד[חול המועד סוכות	ג]ד[חהס'
5th day	19 Tishri	ד]ד[חול המועד סוכות	ד]ד[חהס'
6th day	20 Tishri	ה]ד[חול המועד סוכות	ה]ד[חהס'
Seventh day of Sukkot	21 Tishri	Ho-sha-nah Rab-bah הושענא רבא	
Eighth day of Sukkot	She-mi-ni A-tse-ret Sim-chat Torah 22 Tishri	שמיני עצרת שמחת תורה	

23 Tishri (after sunset, before midnight) Mo-tsei Sukkot מוצאי סוכות

| First day after Sukkot | Is-ru Chag Sukkot 23 Tishri | אסרו חג]ד[סוכות | אח'ן]ד[ס |

Appendix B. Translations of Epitaphs in Hamadrikh

Hamadrikh

Hamadrikh[28], the best known of the Rabbi's Guides has a section on inscriptions, but without translation. Those inscriptions are now among the most common that are found on post 1940 monuments, because of the ubiquity of this book. This section provides both the text and translation of these inscriptions.

These inscriptions tell a story about the deceased. They characterize the individual as young or old, leader, worker, generous, etc. But while these inscriptions may tell a general story about the deceased, they give very little specific information.

Rabbinic Inscription #1:

English	Transliteration	Hebrew
The crown of our head has died.	na-fe-lah a-te-ret ro-shei-nu	נפלה עטרת ראשנו
Our teacher and rabbi has left us.	a-zav o-ta-nu mo-rei-nu ve-ra-bei-nu	עזב אותנו מורנו ורבנו
Surely every member of our community will weep.	ba-cho tiv-keh kol ke-hal a-da-tei-nu	בכה תבכה כל קהל עדתנו
Woe unto us, that our glory (literally: sun) has departed:	Oi na la-nu ki shak-a shim-sho-tei-nu	אוי נא לנו כי שקעה שמשתנו
our master and sage, the great rabbi....	ma-ra-nan ve-ra-ba-nan ha-rav ha-ga-dol...	מרנן ורבנן הרב הגדול...

Rabbinic Inscription #2:

English	Transliteration	Hebrew
A shepherd of a holy congregation,	ro-eh a-dat ke-do-shim	רועה עדת קדושים
he taught wisdom	ho-reh dei-ah	הורה דעה
and understood halachah.	ve-hei-vin she-mu-ah	והבין שמועה
He led with knowledge	bi-te-vu-na na-hal	בתבונה נהל

---

[28] Goldin, *Hamadrikh*, (Hebrew Publishing Co., New York, NY, 1939)

a congregation of Jeshurun (Israel).	ke-hal a-dat ye-shu-run	קהל עדת ישורון
And he led them in the ways of	Ve-yad-ri-cham be-or-chot	וידריכם בארחות
Torah and ethics.	To-rah u-mu-sar	תורה ומוסר
Justice and righteousness	Mish-pat u-tse-da-ka	משפט וצדקה
he did among his people.	a-sa be-a-mav	עשה בעמיו
The great rabbi, master and sage	ha-rav ha-ga-dol ma-ra-na ve-ra-ba-na	ה"ה מרנא ורבנא
the brilliant rabbi...	ha-rav ha-ga-on...	הרב הגאון...

The Wise and God Fearing:

Wisdom is a basic Jewish value. The "Ethics of the Fathers" (2:6) states that an ignoramus cannot be righteous. The following inscriptions stress the importance of wisdom.

Wisdom: Inscription #1:

A perfect and upright man,	Ish tam ve-ya-shar,	איש תם וישר
and he feared God.	ve-ya-rei ha-shem	וירא ה'
All his days, he dedicated	Kol ya-mav hik-dish	כל ימיו הקדיש
time for Torah	ei-tim la-to-rah	עתים לתורה
and worship.	ve-la-a-vodah.	ולעבודה.
His good deeds	Ma-a-sav ha-to-vim	מעשיו הטובים
and sincerity	ve-ha-ye-sha-rim	והישרים
were known to be praiseworthy.	no-de-u la-te-hi-lah	נודעו לתהלה

Wisdom: Inscription #2:

A man of truths,	Ish e-mu-nim,	איש אמונים
righteous and upright:	tsa-dik ve-ya-shar	צדיק וישר
He served his Maker with	a-vad be-leiv sha-leim	עבד בלב שלם
a full heart.	et ko-no	את קונו
Of his riches he gave	u-mei-ho-no na-tan	ומהונו נתן
to the poor;	le-ev-yo-nim	לאביונים

178

and for the study of	u-le-ha-got	ולהגות
the Torah of God	To-rat ha-shem	תורת ה'
he dedicated his time.	hik-dish i-to-tav	הקדיש עתותיו

A Philanthropist:

A number of wealthy Jews choose to be philanthropists. The Jewish ethic or mitsvah of *tsedakah* encourages this practice. The sample inscriptions that follow acknowledge the practice.

Philanthropist: Inscription #1:

A righteous man,	Ish tsa-dik	איש צדיק
observer of truths,	sho-mer e-mu-nim	שומר אמונים
worker for righteousness	po-eil tse-dek	פועל צדק
and perfection;(cf. Psalms 15:1)	ve-ho-leich ta-mim	והולך תמים
He was strength for the	Ma-oz le-dal	מעוז לדל
downtrodden(cf. Isaish 25:4)		
and a refuge to the poor.	u-mach-seh le-ev-yo-nim	ומחסה לאביונים
To do good, he thought	le-hei-tiv cha-shav	להיטיב חשב
night and day.	lei-lot ve-ya-mim	לילות וימים

Philanthropist: Inscription #2:

A generous man	Ish ne-div leiv	איש נדיב לב
and magnanimous:	ve-ya-kar ru-ach	ויקר רוח
He did charitable works	Tse-da-kot a-sa	צדקות עשה
in Israel.	be-yis-ra-eil	בישראל
He loves fellow humans	o-heiv ha-be-ri-ot	אוהב הבריות
and was a father to orphans.	ve-av la-ye-to-mim	ואב ליתומים
He worried about	Do-eig le-a-ni-yei	דואג לעניי
the poor of his people	a-mo	עמו
until the last day.	ad yom ha-a-cha-ron	עד יום האחרון

A Leader of His Congregation:

In North America, most congregations are affiliated with a larger national or international group. Lay leadership is organized by the local congregation and usually includes a president and a board of directors.

In other countries, congregations are organized differently. Sometimes their titles find their way to the cemeteries when they reach other countries. In America, the terms *Parnas* and *Gabai* are used, but in a much less formalized hierarchy. Several standard epitaphs for congregation leaders follow:

Leader of a Congregation: Inscription #1:

He was a man who seeks	Ish do-reish	איש דורש
good for his people	tov le-a-mo	טוב לעמו
and works righteously	u-fo-eil tse-dek	ופועל צדק
within his community.	be-ei-da-to	בעדתו
His soul clung	naf-sho da-ve-ka	נפשו דבקה
to the living God	bei-lo-him cha-yim	באלהים חיים
and all his deeds were	ve-chol ma-a-sav ha-yu	וכל מעשיו היו
for the sake of heaven.	le-sheim sha-ma-yim.	לשם שמים
(Avot 2:17)		
This man was the	ha-ish ha-zeh rosh	ה"ה ראש
head of the congregation	ha-ei-dah	העדה
and a beloved leader.	U-man-hig ha-ya-kar	ומנהיג היקר

Leader of a Congregation: Inscription #2:

He was a wise	Ish cha-cham	איש חכם
and beloved man,	ve-ya-kar	ויקר
praised among	me-hu-lal	מהולל
his people,	be-ke-rev a-mo	בקרב עמו
honored among VIPs,	pe-eir i-shim	פאר אישים
and very talented.	ve-kish-ron me-a-le-lim	וכשרון מעללים
His memory will not perish	zich-ro lo ya-suf	זכרו לא יסוף

180

English	Transliteration	Hebrew
for ever and ever.	le-dor do-rim	לדור דורים
This man was	ha-ish ha-zeh	ה"ה
the head of the congregation	rosh ha-ei-dah	ראש העדה
and a leader of the community.	U-man-hig ha-ka-hal	ומנהיג הקהל

A Young Man:

A Young Man: Inscription #1:

English	Transliteration	Hebrew
He was a beloved young man	E-lem ya-kar	עלם יקר
and a pleasant and	u-va-chur nech-	ובחור נחמד
cultured youth.	mad u-mas-kil	ומשכיל
His deeds were recognized	be-ma-a-la-lav	במעלליו
	hit-na-keir	התנכר
because he was pure and righteous.	ki zach ve-ya-shar hu	כי זך וישר הוא
But alas, suddenly,	ach ha pit-om	אך הה פתאום
the hope of his parents was shattered	av-da tik-vat ho-rav	אבדה תקות הוריו
for he died an untimely death.	ki ve-lo i-bo ke-ta-fa-hu ha-ma-vet	כי בלא אבו קטפהו המות

A Young Man: Inscription #2:

English	Transliteration	Hebrew
You were young.	A-le-cha rach sha-nim	עליך רך שנים
We wail and lament	na-sa ne-hi ve-ki-na	נשא נהי וקינה
because your candle was	Ki neir-cha ka-va	כי נרך כבה
extinguished in your youth.	be-lo i-be-cha	בלא אבך
How great is the tragedy	Ma ga-dol ha-she-veir	מה גדול השבר
to your parents	le-ho-re-cha	להוריך
and those who love you.	ve-o-ha-ve-cha	ואוהביך
Is there pain like	Ha-yeish meich-ov	היש מכאוב
our pain?	ke-mach-o-vei-nu	כמכאובנו
For your days never reached	Ki ya-me-cha lo hi-gi-u	כי ימיך לא הגיעו
the years of manhood.	li-she-not ge-ver	לשנות גבר

181

A Boy:

A Boy: Inscription #1:

He was a young boy,	ye-led rach be-sha-nim	ילד רך בשנים
a boy charming	ye-led nech-mad	ילד נחמד
and pleasant.	ve-na-im	ונעים
Because of your death	al mo-te-cha naf-she-cha	על מותך נפשך
tears (flow) like water.	de-ma-ot ka-ma-yim	דמעות כמים

A Boy: Inscription #2:

Your days were few	Ya-me-cha me-a-tim ve-lo	ימיך מעטים
and you did not see good.	ra-i-ta ve-to-vah	ולא ראית בטובה
You went to your	ha-lach-ta le-o-la-me-cha	הלכת
world pure	na-ki	לעולמך נקי
from all sin and obligation.	mi-kol chet ve cho-vah	מכל חטא וחובה
Quickly you ascended	Chish la-ma-rot	חיש למרום עלית
to the heights,	a-li-ta	
a favorite son.	ye-led sha-a-shu-im.	ילד שעשועים

A Woman:

The inscriptions for women that follow are less generous than inscriptions for men. There are none that stress leadership beyond her family. Even the quantity is less. Of the 18 inscriptions in "Hamadrikh", 12 are for men and boys, but only six are for women and girls.

A Woman: Inscription #1:

The woman favored	Ha-i-sha cho-ne-net	האשה חוננת
the poor	da-lim	דלים
and feared God.	ve-yir-at e-lo-him	ויראת אלהים
With wisdom and knowledge	be-hes-keil va-da-at	בהשכל ודעת
she guided her children.	had-ri-cha et ba-ne-ha	הדריכה את בניה
To the poor and downtrodden	le-o-ni ve-ev-yon	לעני ואביון
she extended her hand.	pir-sah ka-pe-ha.	פרשה כפיה.

182

A Woman: Inscription #2:

She was a woman of valor,	Ei-shet cha-yil	אשת חיל
the crown of her husband	a-te-ret i-sha	עטרת אישה
and the glory of her children.	ve-tif-e-ret ba-ne-ha	ותפארת בניה
Righteousness and truth	che-sed ve-e-met	חסד ואמת
and charity	u-tse-da-ka	וצדקה
she did all her days.	ga-me-la kol ya-me-ha	גמלה כל ימיה
She passed away	ha-le-cha le-o-la-ma	הלכה לעולמה
in the prime of her years,	be-miv-char she-no-te-ha	במבחר שנותיה
to the sorrow of her husband,	le-i-tsa-von i-sha	לעצבון אישה
her parents and those	ho-re-ha ve-yo-de-ha	הוריה ויודעיה
who knew her.		

A Woman: Inscription #3, Death in Childbirth:

Today this is relatively rare. Fifty years ago, it was more common.

The woman feared	Ha-i-sha yir-at	האשה יראת
God	e-lo-him	אלהים
and favored the poor.	ve-cho-ne-net da-lim	וחוננת דלים
She departed from life	Sha-ve-ka cha-yim	שבקה חיים
	le-kol chai	לכל חי
in the prime of her years	be-miv-char she-no-te-ha	במבחר שנותיה
and in the pain of her	u-ve-hak-shu-tah	ובהקשותה
giving birth[29]	be-lei-da-tah	בלדתה
in the middle of her life.	ba-cha-tsi ya-me-ha	בחצי ימיה

---

[29] Cf. Gen. 35:17: Euphemistic for death in childbirth as with Rachel

An engaged (betrothed) woman:
Inscription:

English	Transliteration	Hebrew
She was the virgin bride,	Ha-ka-lah ha-be-tu-lah	הכלה הבתולה
modest and righteous:	tse-nu-a va-cha-si-dah	צנועה וחסידה
the joy of her parents,	chem-dat ho-re-ha	חמדת הוריה
and the love of her betrothed.	va-a-hu-vat cha-ta-na	ואהובת חתנה
And all of a sudden,	u-ve-fe-ta pit-om	ובפתע פתאום
she was gathered	ne-e-se-fa	נאספה
to her people (i.e. she died)	el a-ma	אל עמה
before her	be-te-rem bo	בטרם בוא
wedding occurred.	mo-eid ke-lu-la-ta.	מועד כלולתה.

A young woman:
Inscription:

English	Transliteration	Hebrew
She was a young woman,	Na-a-ra	נערה
a virgin,	be-tu-lah	בתולה
modest and pleasant.	tse-nu-a ve-cha-mu-dah	צנועה וחמודה
Like a lily, she died	ke-sho-sha-na be-o-da	כשושנה בעודה
an untimely death,	be-i-ba ka-te-fa	באבה קטפה
	ha-ma-vet	המות
to the anguish	le-da-a-von	לדאבון
of her parents	ho-re-ha	הוריה
and to the grief of	u-le-tu-gat leiv	ולתוגת לב
those who knew her.	ma-ki-re-ha	מכיריה

A Girl:
Inscription:

English	Transliteration	Hebrew
She was young in years:	ra-kah ba-sha-nim	רכה בשנים
a budding lily,	sho-sha-na po-ra-chat	שושנה פורחת
a cruel death	ha-ma-vet ha-ach-za-ri	המות האכזרי
cut off in her girlhood.	be-yal-du-tah ka-ta-fa	בילדותה קטפה
Because of your death	Al mo-teich	על מותך
our eyes cry	ti-zal ei-nei-nu	תזל עינינו
tears like water.	de-ma-ot ka-ma-yim	דמעות כמים

184

Appendix C: Annotated Bibliography

There are quite a few books that include photographs of cemeteries. Many of these are available in very limited quantities and most are hard to find.

The main purpose of this section is to provide a starting point of sources to someone who would like to go beyond the material presented in this volume.

General Information:
Encyclopedias:

The Jewish Encyclopedia(JE), Funk and Wagnall's, Copyright 1906

Universal Jewish Encyclopedia(UJE), New York, NY, Copyright 1941

Encyclopaedia Judaica(EJ), Keter Publishing, Jerusalem, Israel, Copyright 1971

One or more of the three encyclopedias referenced above are available in many public libraries. They are also available in many synagogue libraries. All are highly thought of. Many references to towns, cities and countries have photographs of tombstones. Unfortunately, the photographic resolution is such that most of the inscriptions are generally unreadable. The recommended entries are as follows:

	JE	UJE	EJ
Cemeteries	X	X	X
Epitaphs	X	X	X
Mausoleums		X	
Tombs	X	X	X
Tombstones	X		

The most interesting from a perspective of inscriptions is the JE entry on "Tombstones". A half dozen lengthy inscriptions are presented and translated and there are many cross-references to photographs of the tombstones of famous Jews elsewhere in the JE.

Hamadrikh, The Rabbi's Guide, by Goldin, Hebrew Publishing Co., New York, NY Copyright 1939, 1956

Hamadrikh is a superb collection of customs, laws and services for those who lead Jewish life cycle events. It is well referenced to source materials. Of particular use to this volume are the following pages and sections:

Dedication of a Tombstone: pp. 224-227
Suggested tombstone inscriptions: pp. 246-252
Lists of Hebrew and Yiddish names: pp. 253-263

Abbreviations

אוצר ראשי תבות, (A Treasury of Acronyms) by Shmu-eil Ash-ke-na-zi and Dov Yar-dein, Published by Rubin Mass, Jerusalem, Israel, copyright 1978

This book has approximately 600 pages of abbreviations from the Talmud and Jewish literature. As a result, the same abbreviation or acronym can mean something different, depending on where on the monument it occurs! It is also true that despite the thousands of acronyms and abbreviations, there are some monument abbreviations that are not in the book at all.

Customs

The Jewish Book of Why, Kolatch, A. J., Jonathan David Publishers, Middle Village, Copyright 1981
The Second Jewish Book of Why, Kolatch, A. J., Jonathan David Publishers, Middle Village, Copyright 1985

These two volumes are often referred to collectively as "The Jewish Book of Why, Vol. 1 and 2". It is an amazing assemblage of questions and answers on every imaginable subject in Jewish custom and tradition. For a popular book, it is very well footnoted to source materials. Of particular note to cemeteries and cemetery customs are Volume 1, Chapter 3, titled "Death and Mourning" and Volume 2, Chapter 6 titled "Death and Dying".

The Jewish Mourners's Book of Why, Kolatch, A. J., Jonathan David Publishers, Middle Village, Copyright 1996

This volume, like "The Jewish Book of Why, Vol. 1 and 2" is well footnoted. Some of the material is the same, but a lot of new material is added. While many chapters have material relevant to cemeteries, especially of interest are Chapter 5, titled "The Cemetery Service" and Chapter 10, titled "Graves and Monuments".

The Jewish Way in Death and Morning, Maurice Lamm, Jonathan David Publishers, Middle Village, Copyright 1969.

This volume is a classic that begins at the moment of death and deals with all subject that one might encounter up to interment and beyond.

Dates

The Comprehensive Hebrew Calendar, Spier, A., Feldheim Publishers, NY, Copyright 1981

This book has details of the calendar, which can be used as a supplement to the calendar data presented.

In addition, it has pages with the Hebrew calendar/Gregorian calendar conversions for the period from 1943 to 2100.

Names

<u>The New Name Dictionary,</u> Kolatch, A. J., Jonathan David Publishers, Middle Village, Copyright 1989

There are many volumes that include names, but this is the most complete list. The problem is that the names are presented in alphabetical order in English. However, most people wanting to decode monuments would be more apt to need a list in alphabetical order by the Hebrew letters. For this reason, <u>Hamadrikh</u>, discussed above, has a better section on Yiddish names than <u>The New Name Dictionary</u>, but not nearly the quantity.

Appendix D: Referenced Cemeteries

Appendix E: Seven Stops

During a funeral procession from the hearse to the grave site, Psalm 91 is read by the rabbi. While the custom of "seven stops" is wide spread, one variant of it is as follows. Verse 11 consists of seven words. One stop is made after each word. Each stop is supposed to express reluctance of the mourners to leave the departed one.

Psalm 91:11

For   כי

1st Stop - א   מעמד

His angels   מאלכיו

2nd Stop - ב   מעמד

He will order   יצוה

3rd Stop - ג   מעמד

to you: לך

4th Stop - ד   מעמד

to guard you   לשמרך

5th Stop - ה   מעמד

in all   בכל

6th Stop - ו   מעמד

your ways.   דרכיך

7th Stop - ז   מעמד

Others suggest that the origin of the "seven stop" custom is in the superstitious belief that evil spirits accompany those attending a funeral. Each stop is intended to confuse or shake off one or more of these spirits.

While this custom would normally be a funeral custom rather than a cemetery custom, it is mentioned here, because some cemeteries have markers labeled sequentially: 1st Stop - מעמד א through 7th Stop - מעמד ז. Shown below is the sign for "stop 6" at "Sharah Tfilo, Baker Street Cemetery, West Roxbury, MA."

Appendix F: On Transliteration

Many Hebrew passages are presented in Hebrew, translation and in transliteration.

To be sure, transliteration is an inexact science. The transliteration formula in this book is that used in the mid-1970's publications of the liturgies of the Central Conference of American Rabbis. In the opinion of the author, this is the simplest method for pronouncing Hebrew, by those who really can't read Hebrew.

The transliteration formula for vowels is as follows:
      1. **a** is pronounced as in b**a**t
      2. **ai** is pronounced as in Th**ai**land
      3. **e** is pronounced as in b**e**t
      4. **ei** is pronounced as in v**ei**n
      5. **i** is pronounced interchangeably as in m**e** or f**i**t
      6. **o** is pronounced as in h**o**me
      7. **u** is pronounced interchangeably as in fl**u**te or p**u**t

The transliteration formula for consonants is as follows:

1. The **ch** sound as in the English word **ch**ant <u>does not</u> exist in Hebrew. Whenever **ch** occurs in a transliteration, it is the gutteral sound as in <u>Ch</u>anuka.

2. The combination **ts** is pronounced as in the word ge**ts**. In English, this combination never occurs at the beginning of a word. Therefore, the English speaker, although familiar with the sound, often has trouble pronouncing it at the beginning of a word.

3. All other consonants are sounded as normal English pronunciation.

Appendix G: Why Jews Place Pebbles or Rocks on Tombstones

The material that follows is the most complete treatment the author of this book has ever seen on the subject of "Pebbles," including 37-different reasons. The article is reproduced below with the permission of the author of the article. The only significant changes were making the transliterations consistent with that of this book as described in Appendix F.

Why Jews Place Pebbles or Rocks on Tombstones
by Mareleyn Schneider, Ph.D.
Yeshiva University

Introduction
The Jewish oral and written traditions describe and explain the mundane to the extraordinary, the concrete to the spiritual.

When an undergraduate asked me why did people "deposit" small rocks on graves – notice, he did not use the word "put" or "place" – he opened the discussion to a larger issue.

What in Jewish life gets "deposited"?

First, the focus was on Jewish holidays. On the Jewish New Year, Jews read in Hebrew what is often translated as "God considered Sarah" which has been interpreted as God withdrew Sarah's earlier deposited merits, thus enabling her to conceive a child in old age (in the days before in vitro fertilization). On Yom Kippur, the holiest day of the year, Jews are reminded that each one of them carries a deposit by the Divine in them. By combining that cache with human needs and desires, we seek to help others who are less fortunate. After the Sukkot, the Feast of the Tabernacles, some Jews take their *lu-la-vim* (palm branches) and either put them on the top of the *a-ron* (the ark which encases the Torah scrolls) for collection and later deposit into a grave or simply place them into a garbage disposal unit. On Chanukah, people play the game of *dreidel* (a four-sided top with Hebrew letters) which requires that each player places an initial deposit of coins or candies in the middle of the circle. On Purim, while delivering *mish-lo-ach ma-not* (food baskets) to friends, some parents take their children over to deposit a basket with people who are without means. On the night before Passover, before the ritual of *be-di-kat cha-metz* (searching for bread), Jews deposit bread pieces around the house, before embarking on a hunt for them; the next morning, some Jews deposit any residual bread into garbage cans outside their homes. On both *Tu be-She-vat* (the New Year for Trees) and *Lag be-O-mer* (a minor holiday during a mourning period between Passover and Shavuot) adults deposit goodies for scavenger or treasure hunts. On Shavuot, Jews read and hear about the ancient tradition of *le-ket*, letting any grain that falls to the ground during harvest remain for the use by poor people.

Then the focus of our discussion fell onto what was once colloquially known as the "match, hatch, and dispatch trio". We talked how the eight-day old boy's foreskin – which is cut off after a *brit* – is put into a grave by the *mo-hel* (a man who performs a Jewish ritual circumcision); how a father redeems his first-born son by depositing (often temporarily) five silver coins into a *ko-hen's* (Jewish priest's) hands; how during a Jewish wedding ceremony, the groom deposits the *ke-tu-bah* (marriage contract) into his bride's hands; how, once the deceased is in the coffin, members of the *chev-rah ka-di-sha* (Jewish burial society) place shards of pottery on its eyes and mouth, and sprinkle soil from Israel over the shrouded body; and, how in Biblical times, a year after death, the bones of the deceased were put into stone ossuaries.

After this, our conversation turned to other "deposits": the ancient custom of depositing discarded books and papers with *shei-mot* (God's name) in caves and graves; placing a *lu-lav* (palm branch) on top of a door's ledge until it would be burned about six months later when the *cha-metz* (bread) was burnt before Passover; setting aside an *ei-ruv tav-shi-lin* (a baked item and a cooked item) when a holiday falls on a Thursday and Friday; the relatively new custom of depositing items which require safekeeping – such as cell phones, remote controls – into a box until the Sabbath is over to free Jews from the workday world; and libraries which collect materials of all types which reflect or represent the cultural, economic, and political histories – and achievements – of the Jewish people.

The lesson from this: Since the Jewish people have a long history of depositing things, placing pebbles on tombstones may seem odd, but it is just one example of putting things down or away in Jewish cultural life.

What is the role of stones (which includes gemstones, rocks of all sizes, and pebbles) in Jewish history?
At the behest of God, the patriarch Abraham bound his son on a stone to be sacrificed (an act which was ultimately aborted by

heavenly decree). That stone – known as the foundation stone because it is said to be the center of creation – was the location of the Holy of Holies of the Temple in Jerusalem and is the focal point of many legends. The Decalogue (Ten Commandments) was written on both sides of stone tablets. After the destruction in 70 C.E. of the Second Temple, one of it outer stone walls remains; known as the *Ko-tel* or Western Wall by Torah observant Jewry and as the Wailing Wall by outsiders, it has become a powerful place at which to pray. One of God's 72 names is "rock". The remains of ancient synagogues contain mosaic floors. A celebrated story is how a young shepherd named David slew the giant warrior named Goliath with pebbles. The *ko-hein ga-dol* (High Priest) wore a breastplate made of precious stones. In the Middle Ages, Jews – like their Christian hosts – attributed virtues to precious and semi-precious stones. According to one legend, the stones themselves built the First Temple in King Solomon's time. Another tale describes the magical *sha-mir* (a tiny worm) who cut and shaped stones from a quarry for the Holy Temple and also engraved names on the stones worn by the high priest. The students recounted the miracles related to the rock which gushed water during the Israelite's 40 year stay in the desert; known as the traveling rock or fountain, it accompanied other miracles of food deliveries. A student studying biblical archaeology described how stones – as well as their locations, types, and placements – are important in understanding unrecorded history. Another shared the story from the Zohar – an important work of Kabbalah (Jewish mysticism) – in which a giant lizard killed a dangerous snake which had slithered out of rocks and was about to accost a sleeping man; the rocks play a major role in this lesson. Accounts of anti-Semitism, across the centuries, contained episodes of attacks by rock throwers. While some tell tales of how their elders smuggled diamonds when they escaped oppressive regimes, other recount stories of family heirlooms.

The lesson from this: The Jewish people have a long tradition of personal and religious lore about stones. So, though pebbles on tombstones may at first appear ugly or even a cheap gift, they are but just one more instance of the centrality of rocks in Jewish religious and social history.

Why do Jews leave pebbles or small stones on graves?

The outsider perspective:

1. Those who could not afford marble or granite stones, collected what is known as field stones to mark a grave. If available, some chose non-indigenous rocks – perhaps taken from a park near their homes – as grave markers.

2. It was a custom to build a cairn (mound of stones) to mark a grave, especially if no stonemason was available.

3. The family and/or community were miserly, not willing to be generous with their money or skills.

4. The early Hebrews, who were nomadic tribes and shepherds not skilled in quarrying and stone carving, marked their graves by mounds of stones.

5. In the past, when huge rocks covered graves, they served to guard the graves from predatory animals and grave robbers. A pebble is a relic of the past or simply a habit that has been handed down.

6. Throughout the world are artificial hills which are burial mounds. Because occasionally a stone would fall down from the mound, a custom developed whereby a passerby would replace the fallen rock; this became a mark of thoughtfulness and regard for the memory of the person buried.

7. In the ancient world, people sacrificed animals on altars which were made up of pebbles. Some of these were burial mounds converted for this purpose. Thus, pebbles serve to remind people of sacrifices the deceased made in life.

<u>The insider perspective:</u>

1. It is a form of artistic expression when an artist works within and with the landscape by embellishing the grave and tombstone with rocks.

2. The stone lets others who visit the grave know that someone else has remembered the departed one. For many, this is a great comfort.

3. In the past, a rock warned *ko-ha-nim* (members of the priestly class) to stay away from the grave so they could remain *ta-hor* (ritually pure) and thus be able to fulfill their duties in the *Mish-kan* (Tabernacle) and *Beit Ha-Mik-dash* (Holy Temple). The ritual survives as a token to remind all about the obligations and limitations of this particular group.

4. Some have suggested that visitors who add stones to the mound illustrate that they, as mourners, are never finished building monuments to the deceased.

5. Some maintain it is an individual's way to participate in the mitzvah of *ma-tsei-vah* (setting a stone upon a grave). In the past, each small pebble – not removed by cemetery personnel in charge of maintaining graves as they are today in the United States – were added to the memorial. Yom Tov Zahalon in his *Le-chah Tov* (1577), a commentary on the Book of Esther, recalling a story he had heard, wrote that each of Jacob's sons took a stone and put it on Rachel's grave to construct her tomb.

6. For the patriarch Jacob himself, stones signify even more. In Genesis 28:18-22 and 35:14-15, Jacob used a stone to offer a libation to God. Thus, the placing a small stone (in lieu of pouring liquid) on a stone (the tombstone) signifies to visitors gratitude to the deceased for participation in their lives and to God for His gift of the deceased.

7. The Babylonian Talmud and the Palestinian (Jerusalem) Talmud were written between 200-600 C.E. During and before Talmudic times, public burial places are not mentioned. The most common burials in ancient times were in family tombs located in natural caves or hewn chambers, often approached by a shaft or passageway and closed with a single

stone or pile of rubble. When vaults were unavailable, the earth was hollowed out for a body. The official mourning period officially began when the *go-lel* (the tomb's stone or rubble) was set in place – either at the entrance or on top – to seal it. In the Tosefot (commentary) to Tractate Sanhedrin 47b in the Babylonian Talmud, Rabeinu Tam – a grandson of Rashi – explained smaller stones were set under the edges of the large stone that rested atop a body them so that it would bear down too heavily on the deceased. These smaller stones, called *dof-kim*, which are a symbol of consideration for the departed, are now manifested by upright tombstones as well as stones placed around the grave.

8. Symbolically, the stone suggests the continuing presence of love and memory, which are as strong and enduring as a rock.

9. Because one name for God is "The Rock of Israel," the stone is a reminder of the presence of the Rock, whose "love truly is stronger than death (Song of Songs 8:6)". Rabbi Andrew Straus offers: "Humans need physical acts to express their emotions and spiritual needs. Just as we give presents (such as precious and semi-precious stones) on special occasions, and we confer medals and awards for achievement, we bestow a symbol of God at the grave to the dearly departed."

10. It is now an organic and quiet symbol of a Jewish grave. For example, at Arlington National Cemetery, Ken Poch removes Christmas wreaths from Jewish graves and replaces them with stones. It makes it easier to locate the 2,500 Jews buried among the cemetery's 250,000 graves.

11. During the period when the Ottoman Turks ruled Palestine and the Near East (1517-1917) an Arab was murdered in Jerusalem on *Sha-bat* (the Jewish Sabbath). After the word went out that he was killed by a Jew, the Jews of Jerusalem were told to pick themselves up and leave or they all would be killed. A noted *Kabbalist* (mystic) went to scene of the crime and, deciding he was permitted to desecrate the *Sha-bat* to save the lives of his co-religionists by engaging in a forbidden *Sha-bat* activity (that is, writing), wrote one of the names of God on a piece of paper and placed it upon the body of the dead man. Immediately, the dead man rose and pointed to one of the Arabs standing in the crowd at the

200

scene; the accused then admitted that he had done the killing. Because of this, the expulsion order was cancelled. After this incident, the *Kabbalist* went to the *chev-ra kad-di-sha* (the burial society) and requested his tombstone be pelted with stones after his death. Though he knew he was permitted to desecrate the *Sha-bat* in this case, he still believed that some *te-shu-vah* (repentance) was necessary. In this case, the stoning of his grave would be symbolic of the Biblical stoning penalty allotted to a *Sha-bat* desecrator. The *chev-ra kad-di-sha* refused this request because it would also dishonor him. Finally, they came up with a compromise: They would place, not throw, stones on his grave and institute a custom that all future Jerusalem graves would have stones placed on them as a form of repentance. The tradition eventually spread throughout the world.

12. The stones on the graves serve as both memorials for the *mits-vot* (commandments of Jewish law, worthy deeds) that the deceased performed in their lives as well as indicators that the visitors want to keep the departed one's deeds, ideals, and influence alive by acting in the same way themselves.

13. Jews are taught that burying someone and placing a marker on the grave is an act of ultimate kindness and respect to another. After a person is buried, of course, we can no longer participate in burying them. However, even if a tombstone has been erected, by placing a stone on it, visitors may feel they are still participating in this special *mitsvah*.

14. The stone serves as an eyewitness. In the Bible, Joshua (24:24-28) set up a stone in *She-chem* to serve as an attestant to God's words.

15. When Laban discovered his daughters had left his home, he pursued them and then confronted his son-in-law Jacob. At the end of their conversation and making pledges toward one another, Jacob set up a pillar of stone and also ordered that stones be gathered into a heap. On the other side, his father-in-law said that the heap of stones and the pillar would be witness to a boundary over which neither of them passes (Genesis 31: 20-52) as noted in the preceding reason. Moreover, just as the stones marked the separation of Jacob and Laban, a tombstone (representing the pillar) and a pebble (representing the stone heap) signify the rupture

between life and death, between the living and the dead.

16. An ancient Jewish belief is that a soul continues to dwell, for a while, in the *beit o-lam* (graves; literally, permanent house). One explanation of stones on the grave is to ensure that souls remain where they belong – in the grave – until they move on to the next world.

17. Stones are simply important in Jewish history and life. In the Bible, for example, altars to God – were piles of stones. In one case, when Abraham, following God's instructions, binds his son Isaac for sacrifice, he did this at *e-ven ha-she-ti-yah* (foundation stone of the world). The remaining (outside) wall of the second Temple is made of stones.

18. Jewish Psychoanalyst Theodor Reik (1888 - 1969) maintained – that like people throughout the world who believe that the soul of the deceased haunts the grave for a long time – prehistoric humans used boulders to prevent the dead from escaping and plaguing living relatives. As time elapsed, many small pebbles formed a substitute for the one big boulder. The rocks, then, protect visitors from the envy or hostility of those who departed.

19. The five-letter Hebrew abbreviation (*tav, nun, tsadi, bet, hei*) found on many tombstones, stands for *te-hi naf-sha-to (or naf-sha-tah) tsa-ru-rah bi-tse-rur ha-cha-yim* (may his/her soul be bound up in the bonds of eternal life)". The fourth word of the phrase can also be translated as "pebble."

20. In ancient times, shepherds needed a system to keep track of their flocks. They carried a sling over their shoulder; it was filled with pebbles enumerating the number of sheep in their flock. At the end of the day, they checked to see if the number of sheep matched the number of pebbles; if not, they went looking for the errant animals. Placing a stone on the grave is a way to ask God to keep the departed's soul in God's sling.

21. Unlike both life and flowers which fade – "All flesh is grass, and all its beauty like the flower of the field; grass withers and flowers fade" (Isaiah 40:6-7) – stones do not. Placing a stone on a tombstone reminds us that souls endure and that our memories will never dim as long as we visit our loved ones' graves.

22. A recent innovation: Some now bring polished rocks or minerals, rather than pebbles or small rocks, to engage in *hi-dur mits-vah* (beautifying or enhancing the custom) and honor the departed who embellished all their *mits-vot* in life.

23. Ithak Sperling, in his 19th century *Ta'amey Ha'minha-gim* (The Reasons for the Customs) wrote: "We put grass and pebbles on the grave to show that the visitor was at the grave. It was a sort of calling card to tell the deceased that you have paid him a visit."

24. Another modern take: "When we pick up a stone away from the cemetery and hold it until arrival at the grave, it makes an impression on our hands. This reminds the holder that the departed also left an impression. Every time we visit the grave and pick up a stone, we can feel the deceased's impact in terms of life, love, teachings, values, and morals."

25. Stones – with their placement, sediment, colors, nicks, and veins – have a visual story to tell.

26. Worn over the *ko-hen ga-dol*'s robe were two sets of stones (on his shoulders and on a breastplate) inscribed with the names of the tribes of Israel. Not only did the stones represent the people when the high priest went into the Holy of Holies (or "the presence of God"), but they served as a reminder, a continued memory, of the tribe's existence. Similarly, the two sets of stones today – the tombstone and the visitors' stones – serve as a reminder of the departed's existence.

27. After choosing one member of each tribe, Joshua charged each one with the task of picking up a stone from the Jordan River and depositing it on its banks as they entered the Promised Land. The rocks were to memorialize this miraculous event. Today, deposited rocks serve to remind others that the departed is on the way to another promised land.

28. It is said throughout Jewish history, people have deposited stones to signify a place of memory for them of a settlement's founding, a forced removal, or a death. The stones express stability and permanence; their portability and delivery suggest the ability for humans settle in a fresh

place, ready to begin a new life.

29.   On their travels, some visitors collect pebbles or small rocks. In addition to being inexpensive souvenirs, they trigger memories which result in storytelling about events, heroes, overcoming adversity, and survival. As someone told another: "A person's personal history may be compared to a mixture of mud, sand and stones. But after years of mud and sands being flushed by rains, the wet rocks radiate sparkles from their long history."

30.   Since the 18th century, Chasidic Jewish men have customarily given their *rebbes* (a charismatic leader of a Chasidic sect) pieces of paper (known as *kvit-lach*) which contain their names and the names of their family members to be included in the *rebbes'* prayers. After death, this *minhag* (custom) continues. In addition to pebbles, today many people – men and women of all religious denominations – leave *kvit-lach* at *rebbes'* graves, believing they are a means of "talking" to eternal souls (*ne-sha-mot*) who will in turn intercede on their behalf with God. Some who have seen these papers have speculated that the pebbles were originally placed there as paperweights.

The lesson from this: Like stones, memories of the departed and Jewish culture endure.

Additional References
Frankel, Ellen. The Classic Tales: 4,000 Years of Jewish Lore. Northvale, NJ: Jason Aronson, 1993.
Trachtenberg, Joshua. Jewish Magic and Superstition: A Study in Folk Religion. Philadelphia: University of Pennsylvania Press, 2004.
Vilnay, Zev (ed.) Legends of Jerusalem. Philadelphia: Jewish Publication Society, 1973.

Appendix H: Secular Symbols that appear from time-to-time in Jewish cemeteries

The following list has been culled from many sources.   Many of the symbols named below have Christian, Victorian, pagan, mythological or other non-Jewish sources. Most Jewish cemeteries have rules banning non-Jewish symbols, so when subtle religious symbolisms finds themselves in a Jewish cemetery, the symbolism has usually been re-interpreted as secular.

Acanthus	Plant: Greek and Roman architectural decoration widely used to decorate slabs.
Anemone	Plant: Brief blossoming and early death
Acorn	Strength, The best of the acorn (the oak) grows only after placed in the ground.
Altar	Symbol of sacrifice, worship, thanksgiving and remembrance
Anchor	Hope, Marine symbol signifying hope and an object to cling to for safety
Angel	God's Messenger or on a Child's grave, innocence (See also, "Winged Cherub")
Angel with Sword	Justice

Animals	Lambs: depict the innocence of children.
	Serpents:
	    Part of caduceus indicating the deceased was a physician.
	    With tail in mouth, a Celtic symbol with a similar in meaning to a circle.
	    Also, serpents are trampled in triumph over sin and death (Adam and Eve Story).
	Doves are for the Holy Spirit (*Shechinah*), love, peace, or renewed life.
	See also, other animals by name.

Apples	Sweetness in love
Archway	See Gates

Arrow	Death (American colonists used the arrow to attribute the death to colonial attacks by native Americans)
Axe	Martial Themes
Birds	Free spirit, Flight of the soul
Book	Word of God (Bible), scholarship, wisdom
Branch	See Tree (cutoff)
Breasts	Divine nourishment of the soul
Butterfly	Free spirit
Chain Links	Jeweler Member of IOOF (Independent Order of Odd Fellows). In the latter case, often accompanied by initials FLT (Friendship, Love and Truth)
Chain Links (Broken)	Links of love broken by death
Cherub	See "Winged Cherub"
Circle	The perfect shape, endless, signifying eternity.
Circle (broken)	Break in circle equals end-of-life
Clouds	Transition to heaven
Clouds with Hand	God calling the soul to heaven
Coffin	Death of body
Column (also see: Obelisk)	Freestanding column symbolizes reaching toward the sky and God.
Column (broken)	See "Tree (cut-off)"
Crown	Symbol of sovereignty, honor, glory, crown of learning, crown of Torah
Daisy	Simple decorative design
Dove	See "Animals: Dove"

Drapery	Parted fabric: gateway to heaven (See also Urn with Drapery)
Evergreen	Eternity (see also, Ivy)
Eye	The seeing eye of God
Face of Death	Represents mortal remains: See also, "Winged Head of Death"
Father Time	Inevitability of death
Ferns	Humility (because they grow in shade)
Finger pointing up	Soul gone to heaven
Finger pointing down	God calling soul to heaven
Flame	Light, life, and eternity
Fleur de Lis	Boy Scout logo (unusual in Jewish cemetery because it is also a variant of a cross). It can be made of lilies or irises.
Flowers, general (see specific flowers for more details)	Beauty and brevity of life
Flower bouquet	Grief and condolences
Flower bud	Died young (i.e. unblossomed)
Flower with a broken stem	Life cut short
Fruit	See specific fruits
Garland	Crown-shaped with flowers: Crown = glory; Flowers = transcience
Ivy (evergreen)	Faith, loyalty, patience, immortality and bonding;
Gourds	Passing of earthly things
Grapes	Abundance, fertility

Griffin (Body of a lion with a head and wings of an eagle.)	Power, Guardian, Watchfulness.
Hand (left)	Evil
Hands (pair)	Prayer
Hand (right emerging from a cloud)	A blessing from God
Hands (clasped)	Female hand on the left side and a male on the right. Symbolism: love and friendship not severed by death. Also, God's welcome to heaven and farewell to material life.
Heart	Love
Hour Glass (with or without wings)	Fleeting time, brevity of life
Ivy	Loyalty
Lamb	Innocence (often on the monument of a child)
Laurel Wreath	Victory in athletics or achievement in the arts
Lighthouse	A safe haven.
Lilies (white and pure)	Puriy, chastity, Victorian symbolism for death and mourning;
Mistletoe	Druid symbol: Life and protection
Moon	Rebirth, (symbolism: female cycle)
Oak Leaves	Maturity, died at ripe old age
Oak (see also, acorn)	Immortality, strength
Obelisk	Full life, pillar of the community (of Egyptian origin)
Obelisk (broken)	See "Tree (cut-off)"

Olive Tree	Peace and security
Palm	Usually Christian symbol of resurrection. In a Jewish cemetery a lulav (palm branch) is unusual but would represent uprghtness.
Pansy	Thought
Passion Flower	Sacrifice, suffering and redemption (Strongly Christan and very unusual in a Jewish cemetery)
Primrose	Decorative design
Pomegranates	Fertility and were traditionally worm free
Pyramid	See Obelisk or Column
Ring	See Circle
Rising Sun	Resurrection
Roses (without thorns)	Innocence and paradise, love, beauty
Scroll	When not a Torah, symbol of life and time. Both ends rolled up indicates a life that is unfolding like a scroll of uncertain length and a past and future hidden. Sometimes, the scroll is held by a hand representing life being recorded by Angels. It can also suggest honor and commemoration.
Scythe or Sickle	Time and death. Indicates life cut off.
Serpent	See "Animals: Serpent"
Sheaf	See "Wheat"
Sheep	See "Lamb"
Shells	Life and resurrection. Mythological origins.
Ship	Sea Farer, boat lover
Ship sailing	Died on a ship
Ship sinking	Died in a ship wreck
Ship in a storm	Died at sea in a storm

Skeleton	Represents mortal remains: See also, "Winged Head of Death"
Skull with Crossbones	See "Skeleton"
Snake	See "Animals: Serpent"
Spiral	Movement and progressive development upward. Often appears as an ascending spiral around a column.
Spire	See Column or Obelisk
Stump	See "Tree (cut-off)"
Sun	Life, God
Sunflower	Gratitude and affectionate remembrance. The flower turns towards the sun, indicating brightness
Sunrise	Rebirth or entry into heaven
Sunset	Death
Temple	Usually Masonic
Torch	See Flame
Torch upside down	Extinguished flame. Light for the underworld (Egyptian)
Tree	Creation, Tree of Life: See also specific tree type
Tree (cutoff) or Tree Bole	Life cut short
Urn	The body (i.e. the urn: physical container) for the soul (immortal). Signifies death and mourning.
Urn draped with a shroud or a cloth.	Usually Christan symbolism. In a Jewish cemetery, the cloth is symbolic that the work of life is incomplete and partially hidden (or veiled).
Vase, with or without flowers	Vase = soul (permanent); flowers = physical existence (temporary, wilts, fades)

Wheat	A life completed (i.e. the harvest is completed)
Willow plus Urn	Grief (willow) over earthly remains (urn)
Willow (Weeping)	Sadness, mourning and death.
Winged Cherub	Combines the wings of an angel with the face of a child or cherub. It was a sign of resurrection and heavenly reward and replaced the "Winged Death Head" design in 18th century. It shows up in Jewish cemeteries including the Old Colonial Jewish Cemetery in Newport, RI
Winged Death Head	Common especially between 1680 and 1820. It portrayed "orthodox Puritanism" by stressing decay and the grim reality of death. It shows up in Jewish cemeteries including the Old Colonial Jewish Cemetery in Newport, RI.
Winged Globe	God's ubiquitousness over earth
Wings	Flight of Soul to Heaven
Wreath	See garland

Appendix I: Abbreviations and Prefixes

Everything that appears to be an abbreviation may not be. If the abbreviation for which you are looking is not on the list that follows check first to see if the first letter of the abbreviation is one of those that follows. If it is, look for the abbreviation without the prefix.

Also, many things that appear to be abbreviations are really numbers. For Tables of Hebrew letter numerical equivalents, see chapter 7.

Prefixes:

In, on	ב
Of, belonging to	ד
The	ה
and	ו
As, like	כ
To, toward, for	ל
From	מ
Of, that	ש

Abbreviations:

א

Our father, Abraham	אברהם אבינו	א"א"
My master, my father	אדוני אבי	א"א
So be it (Amen) [but emphatic]	אמן אמן אמן	א"א"א"
So be it (Amen) [but emphatic]	אמן אמן סלה	א"א"ס"
Chief of the Court	אב בית דין	אב"ד
My master, my teacher & my rabbi	אדוני מורי ורבי	אדמו"ר
Our master, our teacher, our rabbi	אדוננו מורנו ורבנו	אדמו"ר
Lover of God	אבבת השם	א"ה
First day after Sukkot (24 Tish-ri)	אסרו חג [ד]סוכות	אח[ן]דס

213

English	Hebrew	Abbr.
First day after Passover (23 Ni-san)	אסרו חג [ד]פסח	אח[ן][ד]פ
First day after Sha-vu-ot (8 Si-van)	אסרו חג [ד]שבועות	אח[ן][ד]ש
Man of God	איש אלהים	אי"א

ב

English	Hebrew	Abbr.
Praise be the Righteous Judge	ברוך דיין האמת	בד"ה
(A blessing offered acknowledging and accepting God's will.)		
In this place	במקום הזה	ב"ה
God willing	בעזרת השם	ב"ה
The synagogue	בית הכנסת	בהכ'
With the help of God	בסיוע השם or בס"ד	בס"ד
Torah reader	בעל קורא	ב"ק
Sounder of the Ram's horn	בעל תקיעה	ב"ת
Son of Mister ...	בן רב	בר"
Also: Daughter of Mister	בת רב	בר"

ג

English	Hebrew	Abbr.
A prominent woman	גברת חשובה	ג"ח

ד

English	Hebrew	Abbr.
God (ד =4 and represents the 4 letter name of God)	יהוה	ד'
Of Rosh Hashannah	דראש השנה	דר"ה
Of the New Moon	דראש חדש	דר"ח

ה

English	Hebrew	Abbr.
God	השם	ה'
The man	האיש	ה'
The woman	האשה	ה'
The young man (over 13 but unmarried)	הבחור	הבח'
The young woman (over 13 but unmarried)	הבחורה	הבח'
The great scholar	החכם הגדול	ה"ה

English	Hebrew	Abbr.

The honored sir.   האדון הנכבד   הד'

Note: The abbreviation offers the possibility of any noun/adjective combination. There are many other possibilities.

He (She) passed away   הלך לעולמו(לעולמה)   הל'

The modest one   הצנועה   הצנ' or הצ'

The sainted Rabbi   הרב הצדיק   הרה"ץ

ז

May his(her) memory be a blessing   זכרונו(זכרונה) לברכה   ז"ל

His merit will protect us   זכותו יגן עלינו   זי"ע

May the memory of the righteous be a blessing.   זכר צדיק לברכה   זצ"ל

ח

Intermediate day (of a festival)   חול המועד   חה'

Intermediate day of Sukkot   חול המועד סוכות   חהס'

Intermediate day of Passover   חול המועד פסח   חהפ'

Intermediate day (of a festival)   חול המועד   חוהמ'

Intermediate day (of a festival)   חול המועד   חוהמ'

Act of true kindness   חסד של אמת   חש"א

(often associated with the work of a Chev-rah Kad-di-sha)

י

fears God   ירא אלהים   י"א

God fearing   יראת אלהים

He will rest in peace   ינוח בשלום על משכבו   יבע"מ

(from "Eil ma-lei ra-cha-mim" prayer)

Day of Atonement (10 Tish-ri)   יום כפור   יכ"

Little Day of Atonement   יום כפור קטן   יכ"ק

Day   יום   יו"

His (her) soul departed   יצא(ה) נשמתו(נשמתה)   י"נ

May God guard him   ישמרהו צורו וגואלו   יצ"ו

Fears of heaven (i.e. God)   יראת שמים   יר"ש

כ

The honored …	…כבוד	כ'…
The honored sir	כבוד האדון	כ'ה'
The honored rabbi	כבוד הרב	כ'ה'
Our honored master, scholar, rabbi	כבוד מורנו החכם ור' רבי	כמהור"ר
The Righteous Priest	כהן צדיק	כ"ץ
his name was my pride.	כבוד שמו תפארתי	כשת"י

ל

| By the Jewish Calendar (full) | לפרט גדול | לפג" |
| By the Jewish Calendar (minor) | לפרט קטן | לפק" |

(i.e. a year, such as 5760 is represented by 760)

מ

Mr.	מר	מ"
Mrs.	מרת	מ"
Our teacher & rabbi	מורינו הרב	מו"ה
See כמהור"ר		מהור"ר
After Yom Kippur	מוצ' יו' כפ' מוצאי יום כפור	

(11 Tish-ri after sunset, before midnight)

| Saturday after sunset | מוצ' ש מוצאי שבת | |
| Me-na-chem Av (month) | מנחם אב | מנ"א |

or מנ' אב

or מ'אב or מ'א

from the city of...	מעיר	מע'
from the holy city of...	מעיר הקדוש ...	מעהיק
Place of the grave of...	מקום קבר ...	מ"ק
Mrs.	מרת	מר"
Saturday after sunset	מוצאי שבת קודש	משק

נ

Died	נפטר or נפל	נ"
May his light shine	נרו יאיר	נ"י
All of the following are euphemisms for dying and possible meanings for:		נל"וע
Departed for his eternal home.	נפטר לבית עולמו	
Departed for her eternal home.	נפטרה לבית עולמה	
Departed for paradise.	נפטר(ה) לגן עדן	
Departed for eternal life.	נפטר(ה) לחיי עד	
May his (her) rest be Eden	נוחו(נוחה) עדן	נ"ע
Died	נפטר	נפ"
Here lies	נקבר(ה) פה	נ"פ

ס

Sukkot	סוכות	ס'
The Levite (Literally: Assistant to the priesthood)	סגן לכהונה	סגנ"ל
The Levite (Literally: Assistant to the priests)	סגן לכהנים	סגנ"ל
The Levite (Literally: Assistant to the leadership)	סגן לוי	סגנ"ל
The Levite (Literally: Assistant to the leadership)	סגן ללויה	ס"גנל
Pure Sephardic (Spaniard)	ספרדי טהור	ס"ט
Scribe of Torah -Tephillen, Mezzuzot	סופר תורה תפלין מזזות	סת"ם

ע

Eve of	ערב	ע'
Eve of Yom Kippur (9 Tish-ri)	ערב דיום כפור	עד"יכ
Eve of Sukkot (14 Tish-ri)	ערב דדסוכות	עדס'
Day before Passover (14 Ni-san)	ערב דפסח	עדפ'
Eve of Rosh Hashannah	ערב דראש השנה	עדר"ה
Day before Shavuot (5 Si-van)	ערב דשבועות	עדש'
Rest in Peace	עליו(עליה) השלום	ע"ה
Eve of Yom Kippur (9 Tish-ri)	ערב יום כפור	עי"כ
Eve of Sukkot (14 Tish-ri)	ערב סוכות	עס'

Day before Passover (14 Ni-san)	ערב פסח	עפ'
Eve of Rosh Hashannah	ערב ראש השנה	ער"ה
Eve of New Moon	ערב ראש חדש	ער"ח
Friday	ערב שבת	עש
Day before Shavuot (5 Si-van)	ערב שבועות	עש

פ

Passover	פסח	פ"
President and leader (of the local community)	פרנס ומנהיג	פומ"
Here lies (masc.)	פה טמון	פ"ט
Here lies (fem.)	פה טמונה	פ"ט
Here rests	פה מנוה, or פה מנוח(ה)	פ"מ
Here lies	פה נקבר(ה)	פ"נ
Here lies (masc.)	פה נטמן	פ"נ
Here lies (fem.)	פה נטמנה	פ"נ

צ

| Fast of Gedaliah (3 Tish-ri) | צום גדליה | צג' |

ק

| Honored Mrs. | קדוש מרת | ק"מ |
| Holy Congregation | קהלה קדושה | ק"ק |

ר

Mister	רב	ר"
Rosh Hashannah	ראש השנה	ר"ה
New Moon	ראש חדש	ר"ח

<u>ש</u>

Saturday	שבת	ש'
Ritual slaughterer (of kosher animals)	שוחט ובדוק	שו"ב
(Who) departed from life	שבק חיים לכל חי (ש)שחלי"ח(ש)	(ש)שחלי"ח(ש)
(Literally: Abandoned life for all life)		
She-mi-ni A-tse-ret (22 Tish-ri)	שמיני עצרת	ש"ע
Prayer leader	שליח צבור	שי"ץ
Saturday	שבת קודש	שי"ק
Sim-chat To-rah (23 Tish-ri)	שמחת תורה	ש"ת

<u>ת</u>

She will rest in peace	תנוח בשלום על משכבה	תבע"מ
(from *"Eil ma-lei ra-cha-mim"* prayer)		
Let it be his (her) rest	תהי מנוחתו (מנוחתה)	ת"מ
Jewish Bible: Torah, Prophets, Writings	תורה נבאים כתובים	תנ"ך
Let his (her) soul be	תהי נפשו (נפשה) צרורה	תנ'צב'ה'
bound up in the bonds of the living.	בצרור החיים	

223